Consumer Detox

 **Less Stuff, More Life**

Mark Powley

ZONDERVAN®

ZONDERVAN.com/
AUTHORTRACKER
follow your favorite authors

ZONDERVAN

Consumer Detox
Copyright © 2010 by Mark Powley

This title is also available as a Zondervan ebook. Visit www.zondervan.com/ebooks.

This title is also available in a Zondervan audio edition. Visit www.zondervan.fm.

Requests for information should be addressed to:
Zondervan, *Grand Rapids, Michigan 49530*

Library of Congress Cataloging-in-Publication Data

Powley, Mark.
    Consumer detox : less stuff, more life / Mark Powley.
       p. cm.
    Includes bibliographical references.
    ISBN 978-0-310-32475-1 (softcover)
    1. Consumption (Economics) — Religious aspects — Christianity. I. Title.
  BR115.C67P69 2010
  241'.68 — dc22
                                                         2010019077

All Scripture quotations, unless otherwise indicated, are taken from the Holy Bible, *Today's New International Version™, TNIV®.* Copyright © 2001, 2005 by Biblica, Inc.™ Used by permission of Zondervan. All rights reserved worldwide. Scripture quotations marked NIV are taken from the Holy Bible, *New International Version®, NIV®.* Copyright © 1973, 1978, 1984 by Biblica, Inc.™ Used by permission of Zondervan. All rights reserved worldwide. Scripture quotations marked MSG are taken from *The Message.* Copyright © by Eugene H. Peterson 1993, 1994, 1995, 1996, 2000, 2001, 2002. Used by permission of NavPress Publishing Group. Scripture quotations marked NRSV are taken from *New Revised Standard Version of the Bible,* copyright © 1989 by the Division of Christian Education of the National Council of Churches of Christ in the United States of America, and are used by permission. All rights reserved. Scripture quotations marked NLT are taken from the *Holy Bible: New Living Translation,* copyright © 1996. Used by permission of Tyndale House Publishers, Inc., Wheaton, Illinois 60189. All rights reserved.

Any Internet addresses (websites, blogs, etc.) and telephone numbers printed in this book are offered as a resource. They are not intended in any way to be or imply an endorsement by Zondervan, nor does Zondervan vouch for the content of these sites and numbers for the life of this book.

Cover design: Faceout Studio
Cover photography or illustration: Faceout Studio
Interior design: Beth Shagene

Printed in the United States of America

---

10 11 12 13 14 15 /DCI/ 23 22 21 20 19 18 17 16 15 14 13 12 11 10 9 8 7 6 5 4 3 2 1

▌Praise for *Consumer Detox*

This book is not about guilt. It's about life. Many of us think we are alive, but we are really just breathing. The things we own begin to control us like heroin, or demons. Our possessions possess us, and we find that the more we buy the less we become. We end up the wealthiest and loneliest people in the world. In this book, Mark Powley exorcises the demons of consumerism and invites us to detox from our addiction to Mammon. Mark refuses to accept the lie that happiness must be purchased.

Shane Claiborne
bestselling author, activist, and recovering sinner

At the heart of our current environmental, societal and financial crisis is a spiritual disease: the Western addiction to "stuff." In such a context, *Consumer Detox* is an important and urgent message. However, Mark Powley is not a prophet of doom — his message is refreshingly practical and hopeful, offering a manifesto for a more celebratory lifestyle. Count me in!

Pete Greig
Alpha International / 24-7Prayer.com

Mark Powley tackles one of the most important challenges facing Christian discipleship in the West today with a deep understanding of both contemporary culture and Christian faith. This book is readable, clever, funny, and full of simple, practical, but radical wisdom. If the church took this agenda seriously, it could make a big difference.

Dr Graham Tomlin
dean of St Mellitus College, London

Mark Powley is a leader in a new generation of reliable guides offering twenty-first-century wisdom. *Consumer Detox* will make you laugh, but it's deadly serious — you may need to read it more than you realise. It refuses the dominant operating system of urban cultures in the West, but not in a reactionary or moralistic way. You will not be made to feel guilty or inadequate. No, you will be invited to live your life by a bigger story. You will be offered a grace-fuelled vision for a flourishing life free of the deadening opiate of consumer materialism. I believe there is no more important a book for urban disciples determined to live a real life in obedience to Christ.

Simon Downham
vicar and senior pastor at St Paul's Hammersmith

I don't often finish Christian books, but I couldn't put this one down! It made me laugh out loud and shake my head in disbelief at some of the real-life stories. As I finished the detox, I didn't feel guilty, but challenged and excited—it's all achievable! Every Christian should read this book.

Perry May Ward
contributing author of Simplicity, Love & Justice

Powley is a physician. Surrender yourself to the messages of this book and you will be healed of a disease which has eaten the hearts of millions.

Simon Walker
Leadership Community

Mark Powley has hit the nail on the head with this book. There are few things more pressing than the need for Christians to wrestle with what it means to follow Jesus in our consumer-driven culture, and I'm excited that Mark has found a way to help us do this: a way that is thought-provoking and uncomfortable at times, but also inspiring and practical and that ultimately points us to a better way to live. Read this book, discuss it with others, put some of its suggestions into practice, and you won't regret it.

Ruth Valerio
author of L Is for Lifestyle: Christian Living That Doesn't Cost the Earth

Mark Powley has noticed what is going on in our culture and offers us a real, yet astounding way to live. *Consumer Detox* is crackling with life, full of insight, informative and yet non-judgemental. In a world where Lady Gaga is offering to change the world "one sequin at a time," *Consumer Detox* brilliantly opens up a richer, fuller vision of how to live so we can be alive, generous and free.

Rev. Dr Viv Thomas
director of Formation and Teaching, pastor at St Paul's Hammersmith

Consumer Detox is a great book—accessible, tender, personal and moving. It avoids being preachy because Mark honestly explains his own struggles. At the same time, and more importantly, it is also subversive of our materialist values and very challenging because it shows what it means to claim to be a Christian.

Dr Alastair Duke
specialist in the European Reformation

||||||||||||||||||||||||||||||||||||||||||||||||||||||||

For Jonah, Zach, Nathan, and Sophie

Contents

Introduction

Hi, my name is Mark ... and I am a consumer.

[applause]

It started when I was only little. My parents were both ... consumers. And my two older sisters. And all my friends. Looking back, I guess I didn't have a chance!

Like many of you, I started on the soft stuff. Sweets, football stickers, action toys. But before long, I got in deeper. There were branded clothes, computer games, shopping on weekends. By the time I realized what was going on, it was too late – I was hooked.

Despite living in one of the world's wealthiest nations, it never seemed enough. I found myself daydreaming about my next purchase. I couldn't watch a TV show without taking a commercial break.

Then recently I hit rock bottom: I sold my soul to the system and tried to become a celebrity author ...

|||||||||||||||||||||||||||||||||||||||||||||||||||||||||||||||||||||||||||||||||||

We live in a consumer culture. Consumerism, the lifestyle based on shopping and choice, is everywhere. It's happening right now. Here I am trying to sell this book, and here you are consuming it. (Blast! So much for anticonsumerism!)

Consumerism is *the* great force shaping our society. We don't just happen to go shopping from time to time – it has become central to our identity. We form our lives by the choices we make. We *are* consumers.

But why do many of us consume beyond our means?

How come we have so much stuff but often it doesn't make us any happier?

What's the cost of consumerism to our lives, our communities and our planet?

How can we get beyond a consumer mentality to what's really important in life?

If ever there was a time for Consumers Anonymous it is now. We need our own 12-step programme to break us out of the worst effects of the consumer lifestyle. And we need to work out what freedom looks like. That's what this book is about.

But I should come clean at the start.

I am a consumer. I am, I imagine, like you. I have my doubts about the way the world is working. I know that millions are starving while I have more than I need. But often I'm not sure what to do about this.

I'm not pursuing a life of total simplicity. I don't live with complete strangers in a communal house that we've woven together out of things we found at a dump. I have a car. I occasionally eat at McDonald's. I have been known to associate with advertising executives. I am part of this consumer society.

So this book is not a list of fifty naughty things you should feel guilty about. It's not an anticapitalist manifesto (Mark Powley for world president). It's not a hero story of how I beat The Market single-handedly and now live with chickens.

This is a book by a consumer for consumers. It's written by someone who's learning about generosity, experimenting with simplicity, walking towards freedom.

And more than anything it's about grace.

So how do we get started?

PART ONE

Breakout

I Am a Consumer

When I was a teenager, I experienced what I can only describe as raging shoelust.

Like all the other boys in my class, I obsessed over running shoes. As my old trainers started to lose their lustre, I set my heart on a new pair. After school I would go to Discount Daisy's shoe shop just to look at the new trainers with their sleek design features: bright reflective strips, super-cushioned soles, the Nike swish, the Adidas stripes. Deep down, I knew these shoes were special. I had to have them.

On the way home I would scrape my old shoes against the wall to wear them out quicker. Then the bartering with my parents would begin.

When I eventually persuaded them to replace the shoes I had been busy destroying, we would go along to Discount Daisy's and I'd try desperately to steer them towards the most expensive pair ("these ones don't fit right; can I try *those* ones?").

And the purchase – how can I express in print the thrill of the purchase? Words are too poor. At last, the shoes were mine. All that the trainers were, I now possessed. And if I was lucky, I could *wear them home*!

Do you remember this kind of thing?

Many's the time I would find myself, later that day, lovingly cradling my new shoes and flying them through the air like fighter planes.

OK, maybe that last bit was just me.

The point is: something was going on with those shoes. This was about more than footwear. This was about envy, seduction, the thrill of the chase, the power of the purchase, the warm afterglow of conquest and that profound, inexpressible bond between man and sneaker.

It isn't just me (apart from the fighter plane bit, but I think we've established that). We're all involved in this worldwide love affair with stuff. Consumerism has been growing for a while. Since the nineteenth century, industrialization has allowed us to make more and better products. At the same time, individualism has been on the rise. The members of each generation have increasingly seen their lives as a personal quest for self-fulfilment. In the last fifty years, consumerism has gone global. It has become the driving force of our economy, powered by advertising and easy credit. Now, for most of us, it's the air we breathe – as vital to our culture as TV memories are to our childhood.

There are whole books explaining the story of how we got here.[1] But for now, here we are. Consumers in a consumer world. The question is: Where do we go from here?

||||||||||||||||||||||||||||||||||||||||||||||||||||||||||||||||||||||||||||||

▌ The first step

How do we get a grip on consumerism?

Ask a recovering alcoholic. It begins when we admit the problem. The first step on the road to freedom is to acknowledge what's going on. In *The Shape of Living*, Cambridge professor David Ford writes, "Naming is a powerful act.... To name the situation brings it into language. Language is shared, and to find just the right word links our experience to others."[2]

So let's name this. I love my stuff. I think I have too much. My consumer choices influence me more than I like to imagine. I don't like looking cheap or feeling bored. The idea of a less comfortable life scares me. My name is Mark, and I am a consumer.

But if we're going to name this thing, we need to say right at the start that this is much bigger than just shopping. Consumerism is everywhere.

The chances are you didn't make the clothes you're wearing now (unless you're reading this in the bath). It's unlikely that you grow much of your own food. We get what we want by buying it. We are always consuming.

But it's more than what we do; it's how we think. For the consumer, *choice* is everything. We live in worlds of our own choosing. We choose our location, our occupation, our recreation and our religion. We adopt a "lifestyle." We mix and match as we see fit. The customer is king.

No wonder, then, that we find ourselves "buying into" ideas, "shopping around" for churches or "investing in" relationships. We even put our*selves* on "the job market." We think like consumers; we speak like consumers.

Consumerism spills over any boundary we'd care to put around it. Everything seems to have a saleable value, from the ridiculous ("man sells advertising space on forehead") to the ambitious ("name a star for $54") to the downright disturbing ("kidney for sale").[3] Through the wonders of the Internet, we can buy from most places around the world at our own convenience. Unless we live underground, there is no escape from the world of commercial messages, bleeps, texts, 24/7 shopping and the shift work needed to make it happen.

Consumerism is everywhere.

Good monster/bad monster

So then, consumerism is a bad thing, right?

No.

So it's a good thing?

No.

I think we know in our bones it's more complicated than that.

If you're like me, consumerism is part monster, part friend. If we're going to name it well, we need to see both sides. So let's brace ourselves and look at the ugly, slimy side first.

For starters, consumerism is unsustainable. If everyone in the world adopted a Western lifestyle, we would need at least two planets to resource it, and possibly five.[4] This is bad ecology but even worse math. We don't have two planets. Which means I'm living a lifestyle that can't be made available to all (there's not enough chocolate, for starters).

Consumerism has a monster-sized environmental footprint (actually it's more like a trail of destruction than a footprint). The shopping economy depends on us mining and making and shipping and packaging and throwing away more and more stuff. That's a lot of freight miles. It's a lot of shrink-wrap. It's a lot of carbon emissions. This is unfair. When eco-disasters strike, the rich nations of the world will always find a way through. It's the poor nations, despite their small carbon footprint, that increasingly bear the consequences of the consumer revolution they never got to enjoy.

To be honest, even on a good day I find it hard to justify my lifestyle. Apparently, right now around a billion people are going hungry. What am I supposed to do with that fact? I can buy bottled water I don't really need, while one in six people on the planet can't regularly access any clean water at all.

Consumerism thrives on ignorance. I have no idea who made the vast majority of my stuff. I don't know if they were paid fairly. I don't know if their working conditions were humane. All this is often hidden from view. But I am no longer unaware of the kind of things that go on. I know that Bolivian coffee farmers have been mercilessly let down by the unpredictable coffee market that gives us the low prices we want. I know that children on the Ivory Coast have been held as slaves to produce cocoa for nearly half of the world's cheap chocolate. I know that some underpaid workers, like nineteen-year-old Li Chunmei in China, have literally died on the job. She worked in a stuffed toy factory for twelve cents an hour and collapsed after working sixty fourteen-hour days in a row. As Vincent Miller says, "She was worked to death making things that we try not to call sh*t."[5]

The inner accountant in all of us might find this next statistic interesting: The US and UK currently spend a combined total of nearly $600,000,000,000 on their military each year; they give away only about a tenth of that amount. But the size of defence budgets is just part of this. The real issue is *why* we have them. Why do we need the navies and the surveillance and the border measures? Isn't it, at least in part, to protect a way of life that we can't afford to share with others? Put it this way: if the defences weren't there, our privileged lifestyle wouldn't last long. That's why it has been suggested that consumerism is only the surname of the present world order. It also answers to Military Consumerism.[6] Our lifestyle is propped up by military might, whether it is as blatant as nuclear missiles or as subtle as applying political muscle to energy negotiations.

And all the time I wonder what effect consumerism has on our personal lives. Is a good consumer a happy consumer? Maybe not. According to the psychologist Oliver James, the worst side effects of consumerism act like a virus. He has a name for it: *Affluenza.*

> The Affluenza virus is a set of values which increase our vulnerability to psychological distress: placing a high value on acquiring money and possessions, looking good in the eyes of others and wanting to be famous. Many studies have shown that infection with the virus increases your susceptibility to the commonest mental illnesses: depression, anxiety, substance abuse and personality disorder.[7]

We could talk more about this. We could talk about obesity. We could talk about disposable relationships. We could talk about aggressive individualism and the breakdown of community. We could talk about all this stuff, and we could ask how kids are affected by growing up in this kind of society.

Novelist Ben Okri put it like this, "Material success has brought us to a strange spiritual and moral bankruptcy.... The more the society has succeeded, the more its heart has failed."[8]

This is the ugly side of the monster, the dark shadow of the consumer dream.

But at the same time, consumerism isn't without its benefits. There's a cuddly, hairy side to the monster too.

Consumerism has contributed to our prosperity. The power of consumer demand has encouraged more efficient manufacturing, better technology, developments in health care, and more besides. As I write these words I'm sitting, well fed and well dressed (OK, reasonably dressed) in my comfortable study, typing away on a laptop because my job allows some freedom to pursue my passion to write. It can't be all bad.

Consumerism has created jobs. Despite the huge differences in pay and conditions around the world, our consumer lifestyles have created a vast market for the growing economies of countries like India and China. Have so many millions of people ever been lifted out of absolute poverty in such a short space of time?[9] Is it better to starve on a peasant farm or to work towards a living wage in a factory?

Consumerism is allied to great political freedoms too. Who would want to surrender the right to spend freely earned wages on what we choose? Who dares to return to the grinding poverty and rigid inequalities of earlier periods in history? You first!

I am a torn soul. The monster is also my friend. In fact, like every other consumer in the system, I am implicated. I am part of the monster.

Guilt-flavoured ice cream

Not only is consumerism complicated; our reaction to consumerism is complicated too.

On the one hand, some of us feel provoked to outrage. One lifestyle website I saw recently tried to make its point with the following statistics:

- Annual spending on ice cream in Europe: $11,000,000,000
- Annual global investment needed to provide clean water for all: $10,000,000,000[10]

On the face of it, it seems so stark. European indulgence; global need. Then I got thinking: What's the logic here? Is ice cream somehow to blame for poor water supply around the world? Perhaps we should round up all the ice cream sellers, close down the factories, and ban it altogether. It would go underground, like crack cocaine. Ben and Jerry's would be sold undercover on street corners. Would this help?

Let's say we somehow managed to cut out all ice cream spending (without resorting to martial law) and diverted the money to water and sanitation projects instead. Would this really work out? Should wealthy governments administer the funds directly, or would this be patronizing to poorer nations? But if the money is diverted via regional governments, how do we know it will get to the point of need? How many billions in aid have been siphoned off through corruption? Or just misspent? How many sanitation improvements on the ground have later been ruined by natural disaster or war? How many children whose lives have been saved from waterborne disease die only a few years later of malaria, tuberculosis, HIV/AIDS, or famine?

These are tough questions.

I know I'm skating close to the edge here. I need to say right now that the rich countries of the world probably do consume too much ice cream and definitely should invest more in clean water for all. But the stats are never as straightforward as they seem. And a comparison approach can easily lead to an impossible burden of guilt ("This is a great day out we're having—and what a lovely park! Would anybody like an ice cream, WHILE THE POOR CHILDREN OF THE WORLD SUFFER AND DIE?!").

On the other hand, some of us react in the opposite way and end up merely justifying the status quo.

It is often suggested that the world needs consumerism like a car needs fuel. If we don't consume, everything will fall apart, and then we won't be able to help anyone. Or to put it another way, as George W. Bush said in 2006, to save the economy, "I encourage you all to go shopping more."

Actually, this isn't as helpful as it may seem.

Consumerism doesn't always encourage a strong economy. Out of control, it encourages unmanageable debt. We think we're creating wealth, but actually we're just playing with figures on a piece of paper. If only I could illustrate this. If only the economic system could experience a kind of global crash induced by overexposed borrowing.

Hold on ... I've just remembered something: 2008.

What counts as profit on a balance sheet isn't always lasting benefit for society. What happens when the irresponsible debts our society is built on come back to haunt us?

What happens when we total up all the costs of obesity and consumption-related cancer?

How stressed and fragmented is society allowed to become before we ask if it's all worth it?

How much money would compensate for leading unhealthy lives on a degraded planet?

Is this the only way to create jobs?[11]

Where does this leave us? According to David Ford, when we're overwhelmed by something like consumerism, we often suffer from "the wrong sort of guilt and paralyzing isolation."[12] He's right. We feel guilty about the mind-boggling statistics of poverty; yet at the same time, we wonder if there's really an alternative to the current system. And besides, who else really cares enough to change it? So, more often than not, we do nothing.

There has to be more than this. On the one hand, guilt can't change the world. But on the other, I'm fed up with being paralyzed by the idea that the only thing I can do to combat global poverty is buy another pizza.

I'm looking for a way forward. I want to know how to live within the system but without it dominating my life. I want my consuming to become creative, shaping the economy instead of being shaped by it.

I'm looking for breakout.

||||||||||||||||||||||||||||||||||||||||||||||||||||||||||||||||||||||||||

▍Breakout

I'm not the only one.

In a recent UK survey, nine out of ten people said that society has become too materialistic.[13] There are signs in culture too. Chuck Palahniuk's *Fight Club* is one novel that voices a rage against the system:

> You have a class of young strong men and women, and they want to give their lives to something. Advertising has these people chasing cars and clothes they don't need. Generations have been working in jobs they hate, just so they can buy what they don't really need.

> We don't have a great war in our generation, or a great depression, but we do, we have a great war of the spirit. We have a great revolution against the culture. The great depression is our lives.[14]

Somewhere tangled up with all the anger is a cry for something different. I want to give my life to something worthwhile.

But how do we know if this is any more than a fantasy?

How do we know if liberation is possible?

That's when I turn to the Scriptures.

There's a whisper of liberation in the leaves of the Scriptures. There's a conspiracy of freedom. The Bible carries the story of slaves on their way to a new land. It is alive with the songs of those who once were trapped but now find themselves in a spacious place. It's the Scriptures that tell us a fairer world is worth hoping for. They tell us that liberation is possible.

But possible doesn't mean easy.

The book of Exodus finds the Israelites escaping from slavery in Egypt. Previously, they had been caught in the machinery of Pharaoh's empire, oppressed by a system of forced labour and impossible production targets. Now they were travelling across a desert to freedom.

So presumably they were glad to be rid of their old life?

Well, not exactly.

On the way, we catch them moaning to Moses, "If only we had meat to eat! We remember the fish we ate in Egypt at no cost—also the cucumbers, melons, leeks, onions and garlic."[15] It's a tough one, isn't it? On the one hand, we were subjected to cruel slave labour. On the other hand, we had cucumbers. Choices, choices ...

This is what liberation is like. It requires a journey. It means facing the sparse wilderness, and learning some truths about ourselves along the way. But in the end, we will find a new kind of abundance, greater than we have ever known. The path is always worth taking.

Liberation is possible. If we are willing.

Breathe

As for me, I decided I was tired of feeling trapped in consumer culture. I started to dream a different dream with a few friends, and it all came to a head in a conversation with my wife, Ailsa:

Me: One day I'd love to be involved in a movement for simple living.

Ailsa: Why not do it now?

Me: I don't feel I've got it sorted—I'm not good enough.

Unless ...

Unless that was how it worked. Unless it was a group of people united by the fact that they *don't* know the answers—that they've *not* arrived at the destination, but they're willing to go on the journey.

Ailsa: OK. What would you call it?

Me: We could call it Choke, because of the way possessions can choke our lives.

Ailsa: Choke?? Choke?! No one's going to want to be part of something called Choke!

Me: Oh, yeah. Good point. Maybe we could call it Breathe …

And that was how the Breathe network was born. Four friends trying to live differently, seeking inspiration wherever we found it, but especially in the life and teaching of Jesus. Within six months, two of us found ourselves at a Make Poverty History protest in Edinburgh, Scotland, standing by a stall and inviting others to join us. It was the beginnings of an exodus – a breakout. We didn't have the answers. But we were no longer stationary; we had started to move in the direction of greater freedom, larger generosity, simpler living. We had the words of *Fight Club* ringing in our ears and the same hope the Hebrew slaves had. And we had a slogan: Less stuff, more life.

This book distils the lessons we've learnt on the road. Along the way we'll explore what freedom looks like for our consumer habits, our relationships, our communities, and our souls. It shapes up like this:

Part One: Breakout – exposes the workings of consumer culture. We see how it shapes our identity; how it conceals our true wealth; its hidden strategies to make us purchase; and its desperate underlying view of life.

Part Two: Rhythms of Life – breaks the patterns of consumerism. It calls a halt to the world of 24/7, always-on, instant convenience. Instead we explore the rhythm of creativity and rest; the habit of true presence with others; the art of waiting and rich enjoyment; and how to make space for the deeper things of life.

Part Three: Adventures in Generosity – takes us beyond consumerism. It leads us away from the control of money, into radical generosity, and towards a larger vision of the future.

Detox Diary – provides practical steps to break the consumer mould. It has suggestions for each chapter of the Consumer Detox. You could turn to them at the end of each chapter, or save them until the end, or use them to inspire discussions with friends.

The journey

Everything comes back to the journey.

Apparently married couples argue most about money. It's certainly true for me and Ailsa. In particular we have The House Move Argument. This is what happens every time we move house and have to discuss which furnishings to keep and which to replace. It's our tradition to have The Argument just before a major shopping trip. At one time or other, we must have sat in the car parks of most major UK stores having this row.

Here's how it goes:

I think that we can make do with the bathroom cabinet.

I am clearly wrong, because the bathroom cabinet, Ailsa informs me, is hideous. It looks dirty even when it has been cleaned. It must be at least twenty years old.

I say ten.

I am told that this is irrelevant. The cabinet must go.

I seek reinforcements. Think about that really frugal couple we know – would they replace the bathroom cabinet?

But I am outflanked. They are simple-living freaks, and besides, the wife has her hair highlighted all the time. Ailsa has chosen to sacrifice frequent hair colouring for better home improvements. She now has the high ground. And if I'm so keen on simple living, why do I spend so much on holidays and fast food?

I am undone. The truth hurts.

I could go on, but you get the idea.

Money is like this. It causes arguments. It raises all our defences. It plugs into our deepest fears: insecurity, unfairness, suffering, tacky bathroom furniture.

But point scoring and saintly comparisons will get us nowhere. Early on in our marriage, we hit on the journey metaphor, and this has reduced the emotional scars over the years.

The truth is: we're on a journey. One person might be allergic to poor interior design; one might not. I might have a weakness for fast food; you might not. It doesn't matter. It doesn't matter where we're starting from or what pace we're travelling. What matters is the journey.

This is where grace comes in.

Grace says it doesn't matter where you're coming from. All that matters is which way you're facing, and just taking one step at a time.

So I am a consumer. This is where I begin.

How about you?

Can you see this?

Are you willing to try something different?

If so, let's do it. We can embark on a journey to be *more* than consumers. On the way we can learn what it means to *first* be friends and family members, neighbours and citizens, human beings and children of God. If we get that right, "consumers" is the last thing we'll be.

Then when we consume, it will be different. When we consume, we will be more free, more just, more joyful. And sometimes we won't have to consume at all.

This is the breakout I'm looking for.

This is where the journey begins.

CHAPTER 2

▌I Am Not What I Buy

Last summer, in an effort to live more simply, I bought some bargain jeans. There was something a little bit last-decade about them, but I couldn't put my finger on it, and I came home delighted at the good deal I'd found.

But all was not well.

As soon as I got home it began to dawn on me – the jeans were the wrong colour. They were blue. But they were the *wrong* blue. They weren't the crisp azure blue of classic Levi's. They weren't the cool dark blue of subtly fashionable denim. Actually, they were more indigo than blue. And to make matters worse, they weren't faded at all. They were uniformly coloured with a thick navy/indigo hue like … (I'm ashamed to say it) like old men's trousers!

Unknown to me, I had broken an unwritten fashion rule: jeans *should not* look as if they've just been bought, even if they've just been bought. They need, at the very least, to be gently faded in the right places and maybe have the odd scuff mark. I even heard of a store where you can customize your own jeans with wear and tear marks just after you buy them. You pay at the till, then take them over to the scuff machine to vandalize your own clothing.

Imagine this with cars. Imagine buying a brand-new hatchback, then the salesman gives you the keys, and says, "She's all yours. Now here's a hammer and some safety goggles – go for it!"

My experience with the jeans made me realize how fine fashion distinctions can be. It doesn't take much to get it wrong: last season's colours, a poor fit, pristine when it's supposed to look faded or faded when it's supposed to look pristine. The differences are tiny, but when we step over the line, we soon know about it. Something inside us just *feels* uneasy.

What's going on?

More. More is going on than we think. Our clothes have gone beyond keeping us warm and dry. They've gone beyond looking neat or beautiful. Our clothes have become part of a powerful and intricate system to tell others, and ourselves, *who we are*. That's why so much is at stake. That's why it matters if we wear the wrong trousers.

If consumerism were as basic as pure greed or even addiction, we'd be able to grasp what's going on pretty quickly. But the reason it's so hard to quantify, and so difficult to resist, is because it plays on the irrepressible human desire to know who we are.

This is about identity.

|||||||||||||||||||||||||||||||||||||||||||||||||||||||||||||||||||||||||||||||||||||||||

Names

How do I know it's about identity? What makes me so sure?

The clue is this: names. Names are everywhere. Our clothes carry logos; our homes are stocked with brands; the media bring us celebrities.

Adidas, Coca-Cola, U2, Nicole Kidman, Apple, Starbucks, Manchester United, Chanel, Volkswagen, Budweiser, IKEA, Sony, Prada, Google, Rick Warren, Evian, Krispy Kreme, Jay-Z, Michelin, Amazon, New York Yankees, Jack Bauer, FedEx, Greenpeace, Bic.

Even funny things have names. My stapler is called Matador (does it kill animals?). My shelves are called Billy (they're from IKEA – don't ask). My trainers are called Vans. Isn't that odd? My shoes have a name. I don't know what their designer was called; I don't know the names of the people who made them; I don't even know who I bought them from. The people are anonymous. The product has a name. Is that the wrong way round?

Anyway, names are about identity, and we surround ourselves with names.

Why would we do this?

iPod therefore I am

A great shift has taken place in contemporary culture. Our great-grandparents had a much clearer idea of who they were. They were their parents' children. OK, this is obvious, but really they were. They would share their parents' status in life; they would most likely take on their occupation, live in their locality and share their convictions. Identity was wrapped up with things like family, class, background and livelihood.

Who are you? I'm a cotton worker from Bolton. I'm a union man and a Methodist. I'm a fourth-generation Henderson. And so on. When society was more rigid, these identities were pretty fixed. This was understandable, given that most folk were worrying about earning a living, surviving disease and other such things. By and large, there wasn't a great deal of time for identity crises.

But times have changed. Now it's not so important what your breeding is. Many of us change jobs or addresses every few years. We're not expected to follow in our parents' footsteps. So when the question comes, it's much harder to answer.

Who are you?

I don't know.

Ah, but this is the wonder of modern life, isn't it? You can *choose* your identity. You can make your self. In the words of that well-worn phrase, "You can be whoever you want to be."

Great. I can be anyone. How freeing! The world is my oyster.

Where should I start?

Erm, I'm not sure.

Here we are, lost in the social universe, a one-in-six-billion genetic singularity, and we have to solve the puzzle of identity. But we're no longer expected to simply fit into a given tradition. We're supposed to be original. No point just being conventional, right?

Who can help us in the quest for who we are? We're looking for something fresh and unique, something that connects with our need to belong. In return, I suppose we could offer cash. Who can possibly give us a name?

Look no further, consumerism is here. Are you clueless? We've got badges of identity so all-consuming that you'll never wonder who you are again. Are you rootless? We can give you roots: "authentic" clothing labels, hand-cooked potato chips, and vinyl blues LPs. Do you feel disconnected from the planet? Step right up. We've got Gaia beans, herbal shampoo and offbeat holiday locations. Whatever it is that you need to be somebody, you can buy.[1]

This is why the names are so important. They are something to cling to in the identity vortex, names for a nameless culture. Not just one name, but thousands of constantly emerging and fading brands and icons. Out of all this we create a sense of ourselves.

Suddenly, without realizing it, we are what we buy.

How does this work?

Two ways: tribes and trophies.

Tribes

Do you remember how it worked at school? Nobody just drifts through their school years oblivious to others as a fully fledged independent individual. There are groups – tribes. Some school kids identify closely with one group (the football team, the "in" group, the alternative music crowd). Others steer a middle course, connecting on different levels with several groups. And a few just slip through the net entirely.

Now that we're all grown up, though, things have changed. We're much too sophisticated to establish our identity by connecting with a tribe. Or are we?

Being social animals, what if we still do the tribe thing, but keep it a bit more subtle? What if there is still a complex web of tribes, with some of us buying into one tribe, and others managing several tribal commitments, leaving an unfortunate few outside the system?

What could this look like? If I were to map out some consumer tribes, do you think you could find yourself on the list?

I'll give it my best shot …

Consumer Tribes

Fans

Sports fan
Tickets, replica shirts, big TV, beer

Rock fan
Gigs, downloads, alternative message clothing (but not alternative to their social group)

Styles

Fashionista
This season's clothes, magazines (e.g., *Elle*), impeccable presentation, hairstyling and makeup

Sophisticate
Newspapers, novels, theatre tickets, smart clothes, quality regional food and wine

Bling
R & B or rap music, ostentatious jewellery, flash cars, tinted windows

Teenage tribal
At the last count it included: Emos, Nu metallers, Fantasy gamers, Goths, Skaters, Pop princesses, Clubbers and more

Special interests

Sporty/health enthusiast
Sports equipment, gym/club membership, energy drinks

Eco-warrior
Local, organic, recycled, and Fair Trade; do not look immaculate (sign of compromise)

Techie
Computer components, magazines and games, dark/unfussy clothing

Special focus
One all-consuming pastime (surfing, horseback riding, church), happiest in specialized clothing

Roles

Supermum
Invest in things for the kids, food for the family, home improvements, big car

Practical guy
DIY tools, hardy clothes, nothing flashy

Work hard/play hard
City-style suits, expensive socializing, skiing, exotic holidays

Roots

Ethnic roots
Close match to "home" culture, references to cultural icons, free to be different

Country life
Authentic farming gear, practical and well made, off-road vehicles

Urbanite
Mainline fashion shops, trendy but not outlandish, good music and communications technology

Anti-tribes

Middle of the road
Avoid loud branding; use major stores and established products

Dropout
Deliberately scruffy, iconic consumption (films, novels, academic interests)

Unbranded/Excluded
Mismatched or cheap clothes, unhealthy food (or none)

It's an imperfect science, and these are rough examples. But look around any modern consumer society, and you'll see all sorts of these unspoken tribal groupings. Traditions have been replaced by tribes. And all of us establish our identity by finding a place on the map.

Who am I?

I wear Armani suits, holiday in Sydney, drive a BMW and work out at Gold's Gym (Work hard/play hard; Sporty/health enthusiast).

Who am I?

I listen to Beyoncé on my iPod, wear Diesel, eat free-range eggs and give to the Worldwide Fund for Nature (Urbanite; Eco-warrior).

Take your pick. Mix and match. There's a set of names that will just *feel* right (marketers call them "brand clusters"). These are the names that will let us know where we fit, where we belong.

Notice, though, how much it all has to do with what we buy. For almost every tribe, a good dose of shopping can keep us connected to our group and remind us who we are. At least our great-grandparents were paid for their vocations and got their family roots for free. Today identity costs money!

The other thing about these tribes is how hard it is to break out of the mould.

Let's say you wanted to test this.

It's easy. Just try some out-of-tribe consumption and see how you feel. Pick a category from the list that you don't connect with (or, for fun, get a friend to pick it). Then try consuming according to that pattern for even a day.

The truth is that, apart from the odd ironic dabble, outside our usual tribal preferences we just don't feel ourselves. "It's not me," we say. And we mean it. The adverts may offer us individuality, but our consumer choices are actually uncannily predictable. Mark Kingwell comments:

> I can think of no experience in the modern world more unsettling ...
> than this one of realizing that my carefully constructed individuality is as
> transparent and manipulable to a savvy advertiser as if I sported a niche-
> market report on my forehead.[2]

That's why changing our consumption habits is so hard. It's not just that we feel cheap or different when we break the mould. Without our normal branding pattern we forfeit our tribal identity. We feel out of place. Lost.

Trophies

I remember my first year as a teacher. I had a brand-new class of fresh-faced eleven-year-olds. As the year began, they looked up to me with innocent eyes to solve their disputes and soothe the big-school worries away. It lasted about a week.

I remember the exact moment their trust in me crumbled. My classroom overlooked the school car park, and one day I caught some of my class in the middle of a discussion. "We were just wondering which one is your car, sir." I could see them gazing reverently at the headteacher's silver executive model and the art teacher's virile yellow sports car. Surely they're not going to judge a man by the car he drives, I thought. "Mine's the Mini Metro."

How wrong I was.

The Mini Metro was not the British car industry's greatest gift to the world of motoring. And my old red Metro wasn't the most impressive specimen of its kind.

The kids looked out at the little red car. Then at me. Then back at the car. And once more at me, only this time I could almost see the plummeting figures in their eyes as they recalculated my worth as a human being.

I think we all learnt something that day.

They learnt that in the great pecking order of life I was one rank up from pond life. I learnt to park my car round the corner.

And I guess I learnt that this isn't just about tribes. *All* the teachers had cars. This isn't just about what we have; it's about how much and what quality. Having a car is not enough. It must be a car that compares well with others, preferably an attractive, modern car that isn't peppered with rust (I now realize this). In other words, it's not just about tribes; it's also about trophies.

We consume not just to connect with a group but also to establish our place in the group. Trophy consumption marks out who is "the best," who is "good enough," and who needs to make alternative parking arrangements.

Some people aren't that fussed about trophies—what matters most to them is the security of a tribe. But others feel a strong pull to create an identity that is significant or impressive. These are the ones who go for trophies in a big way.

Consumerism, of course, is equally happy with both. It can sell us tribes; it can sell us trophies. Whatever works.

So what trophies are on offer?

Take your pick. Cars, jewellery and houses are the classic trophies. But there are other offers out there as well. You can make a trophy home, through endless DIY or just-so-tasteful furnishings. You can pursue a trophy lifestyle: über-cool surf dude, highbrow book lover, 24-hour party animal. You can pioneer a trophy look—rugged trekker, Chanel chic, muscle-bound (maybe only do one of these looks at a time).

Who am I?

I am a tasteful person (i.e., more tasteful than others); a healthy person (i.e., more healthy than others); whatever my lifestyle is, I do it well.

Even if we're not full-throttle trophy hunters, somehow we all get drawn into the comparison game.

Consider, for instance, how important it can be to wear the "right" names. We're tempted to think that brands and logos don't really mean anything. But that can't be true. Imagine walking into a room and shouting at the top of your voice:

I WANT YOU ALL TO KNOW
I AM WEARING
DOLCE AND GABBANA GLASSES!!

We wouldn't, would we? (Tell me you wouldn't!) It's so crass, so embarrassing. But we do. That's what the writing on the glasses is there for. Like fire safety information by an office door, it's there for a reason. To be read. It's there to tell people, and ourselves, who we are. It's there to say: I am not cheap; I am not out of it; I am OK; I am in.

The thing about trophies, though, is that not everybody gets one. We all know of people who haven't quite made the grade. It could be that their body doesn't "measure up." It could be that visiting their home feels like travelling back twenty years in time. Or maybe they just look plain embarrassing.

Occasionally, a TV makeover programme will rescue one or two of these unfortunate folk by bringing them back up to spec. But the rest serve as reminders to us all. If we want an identity (apart from the identity of being a loser), we need to consume the "right" stuff.

In the end, even against our better judgement, we get sucked into a kind of consumer "arms race." If everyone around us is spending, we have to spend too in order to keep up.[3]

Our consumer choices are "free," but we are not free to buy nothing. We have to keep the trophy cabinet well stocked. We have to keep buying to know who we are.

|||||||||||||||||||||||||||||||||||||||||||||||||||||||||||||||||||||||||||||||||||

▎What's in a name?

It might be that you've got this far and you're wondering: What is so wrong with finding an identity through consumerism? People have always had to establish an identity for themselves; why not do it this way? It's a fair question.

Let's return to names. There are valid reasons to wear a name on your clothes. Conferences, for starters.

But why would we wear *someone else's* name?

An alien visiting planet earth would be confused.

Alien: Hello, I am Alien 3657*¬¬5.

Jeff: That's a funny name!

Alien: Yes. We aliens are envious of human beings like you, Tommy, with your well-developed sense of unique personal identity.

Jeff: Well, actually, I'm not called Tommy …

Alien: I do not understand. Your earth-clothing says "Tommy."

Jeff: Yes, but my name's not Tommy. It's Jeff. I just wear clothes with Tommy's name on them. Tommy Hilfiger? The designer?

Alien: …?

Jeff: …?

Alien: …??

[Uncomfortable silence]

Alien: Where is this Tommy? Do you know him?

Jeff: Erm, no.

Alien: Has he given you his clothes? Is he a generous man?

Jeff: Not exactly … I pay extra money to him so that I can have his name written on my clothes. I also wear the boxer shorts of a man named Calvin …

It doesn't take an extraterrestrial to work out that this is odd. Why would we pay to call ourselves after somebody else? Why would we wear *their* clothes? Why would I want someone else's name on my underpants?

Whether we proudly sport our labels or just quietly know that we've got the right stuff, other people's names have become vital to us.

What is the price of me?

According to sociologist Don Slater, "Consumerism is about continuous self-creation through the accessibility of things which are themselves presented as new, modish, or fashionable, always improved and improving."[4] We make our selves. New things; new me. I can be whoever I want to be.

But what kind of identity results from this?

Consumer identity is changeable. The bewildering variety of names we have available to us is always shifting and morphing. This year's "me" will need updating. But when do I finally know who I am?

Consumer identity is only skin-deep, of course. You can't buy character with cash; it's formed over time. We know this, and no amount of postmodern irony can cover up the fact that any identity capable of being bought isn't worth having.

Consumer identity revolves around one person: me. I connect with the people like me. I compete with the people I need to outdo.

And consumer identity is exclusive. Not just in the sense intended by advertisers (a cut above the rest; exclusive to you our privileged customers). It's exclusive in the *Webster's Dictionary* sense: "Having the power of preventing entrance; possessed and enjoyed to the exclusion of others."

Who is excluded by consumer identity? The poor. They can't get in on the act. They can't afford the tribe or the trophies. They are the unbranded outsiders who don't belong.

If this is the price of identity, who wants to pay it?

Not me.

In the summer of 1995, I was a young student trying to make sense of life and relationships. I didn't know about tribes and trophies. But I knew that there had to be more to life than my adolescent dream of an impressive career (in advertising, funnily enough). I was tired of buying into a consumer identity. And I was tired of trying to make my life fit the glossy image I felt I was supposed to project.

That was when I first heard the Radiohead song "Fake Plastic Trees."

A green plastic watering can
For a fake chinese rubber plant
In the fake plastic earth

That she bought from a rubber man
In a town full of rubber plans
To get rid of itself

It wears her out, it wears her out
It wears her out, it wears her out

She lives with a broken man
A cracked, polystyrene man
Who just crumbles and burns.

He used to do surgery
For girls in the eighties
But gravity always wins

And it wears him out, it wears him out
It wears him out, it wears him out

She looks like the real thing
She tastes like the real thing
My fake plastic love

But I can't help the feeling
I could blow through the ceiling
If I just turn and run

And it wears me out, it wears me out
It wears me out, it wears me out

And if I could be who you wanted,
If I could be who you wanted
All the time, all the time[5]

Fake plastic, fake people, superficial changes that don't last. And underneath it all, rising from the fragments, the haunting refrain: "It wears me out." How true.

Don't we long for an identity that is real and stable and lasting and generous? Isn't this somehow what we were made for? Does anything less than this really do justice to human dignity?

So who am I?

Time for another quote from *Fight Club*: "You're not how much money you've got in the bank. You're not your job.... You're not who you tell yourself."[6]

So who am I then? *Fight Club* continues: you are "the all-singing, all-dancing crap of this world."[7] Is that the answer? We find our identity in exuberant rage against the pointlessness of life.

OK then, how can I do this?

Maybe I'll get into the *Fight Club* DVD a bit more. I could dress sharper, like Tyler Durden in the movie (those shades are so cool), and enrol for jujitsu. Then maybe do a bungee jump. Then I'll really have broken out of the system. Then I'll be the authentic rebel. I certainly won't have just bought into another kind of individualistic consumer identity. Right?

We are back where we began. Back in a harsh and nameless world.

No past, no future, no rules. And the siren voices of consumerism drift sweetly across the waters. Step right up. Whatever it is that you need to be somebody, you can buy.

The reality is: unless we can find some deeper roots for our identity, we'll never be able to break out of consumerism. As long as we're trying to secure ourselves in the social universe, we're at the mercy of whatever tribes are out there. As long as we're driven to make a name for ourselves, we'll never be able to resist the trophies on offer.

But where on earth can we get a deeper identity from?

The Father thing

What if we were willing to accept something radical?

What if there's a voice from outside the consumer system, an identity from a different source?

You may believe this already; you may not. But let's go with it and see what we find.

There's no greater example of a true life than that of Jesus of Nazareth. He knew who he was—more deeply and clearly than anyone who has ever lived.

How could we possibly know this?

From his actions. We know, with great historical certainty, that Jesus moved freely beyond the tribal boundaries of his day. He could eat with wealthy religious Pharisees, but he could also party with known "sinners." He could live without the approval of his hometown peers, and he could reach out to hated Samaritans. We also know that he consistently passed up every kind of trophy that would have advanced him at the expense of others. His story speaks for itself.

But Jesus knew that this was not the way of the world. He knew that most of us, regardless of the religious labels we wear (or don't wear), live like pagans. That is, we live like people who don't know the one true God. We live as if this is an unstable and unforgiving universe. It's no surprise, then, that we end up sticking to our tribes and chasing after trophies.

But Jesus had a different blueprint for life:

> "Love your enemies... If you love those who love you, what reward will you get?... And if you greet only your own people, what are you doing more than others? Do not even pagans do that?"... So do not worry, saying, 'What shall we eat?' or 'What shall we drink?' or 'What shall we wear?' For the pagans run after all these things, and your heavenly Father knows that you need them."[8]

Here's how Jesus saw it. We can live a pagan life if we want. It means concentrating on our own crowd ("love those who love you") and constantly chasing more ("the pagans run after all these things"). This is the world of tribes and trophies. We can live for these things. But it will wear us out.

What if, instead, this is not an unstable, unforgiving universe? What if, through Jesus, we can reconnect with a loving Father? Then a different life would be possible—a life beyond tribes and trophies. A life that explodes the categories of consumerism.

The difference is the Father thing. If the one Jesus called Father can be our Father too, then we can have an identity that's infinitely deeper and more secure than anything anyone could ever try to sell us.

The Father thing is totally unconsumerist.

Why? Because you can't pay for it. No one ever bought a parent. Being someone's child isn't an identity you can make; it's something you're given. It doesn't rest on your personality or performance.

And if we enter into a relationship like this with God, then there really is nothing more to prove to anyone. Our identity becomes the beginning, the source of what we do, not the fragile prize we're always running after.

People whose lives are rooted in this identity become, over time, strangely resistant to consumerism. They begin to love their enemies, and so they're not secured by any tribal group. They live beyond the boundaries of in and out. And they give up the chase for more. Somehow there will be enough for whatever is needed. Someone has whispered in their ear, "Even the very hairs of your head are all numbered."

While any source of unconditional love can help us develop a secure identity, somehow only God's Father-love can truly release this. Simon Walker writes:

> Freedom to live an undefended life involves finding a relationship in which we are safe, secured by an unconditional regard and affection, an unbroken attachment, that holds us despite the threats we face. A relationship in which we are defended by Another rather than by our own strategies.
>
> Human relationships are not big enough. They are not strong enough to survive death, or true enough to give us a proper sense of perspective, a proper sense of ourselves.
>
> What I need is for Another to come and pour into me the love and acceptance I have craved. I need Another to say to me: "I know what you're like, and I still accept you." I need Another in whose presence I feel utterly secure—when I'm with them I don't need to worry about what others think of me or how I appear.... I need Another who is bigger than me, and bigger than all my worries, my ambitions, my needs, my financial anxieties.[9]

If the Father thing is true, if this kind of love actually exists, then it changes everything.

It gives me permission to admit the many ways I've become branded and tried to make a name for myself. And, in a way that will take us the rest of this book to unfold, it shows what freedom looks like.

Freedom isn't when our possessions mean nothing to us. We are physical beings—we will always express ourselves using physical things. But the way we use our possessions can become something different:

Less about finding an identity and more about expressing an identity we've been given.

Less about excluding outsiders and more about welcoming them.

Less about outdoing others and more about empowering them.

Less about having and more about being free to give away.

Now *that* is an identity. That's what I want.

So what is the next step towards it?

CHAPTER 3

I Am Richer Than I Know

On my way out of the train station the other day, I was stopped in my tracks by an eye-catching hardback in a bookstore window. It was the latest title from celebrity hypnotist and lifestyle guru Paul McKenna:

I CAN MAKE YOU RICH

I can see why that title might be attractive. There are worse ways to sell a book than the promise of untold wealth. But what you, the reader, may not realize is that even though I haven't made that claim on the cover of this book, I, too, can make you rich. I have that power. I can use it on almost every reader of this book, even as you read these words.

The question is: Would you like me to make you rich?

Yes?

OK then.

Here goes …

There you are. I've done it.

Unless you picked up this book from a trash bin, I'm more than 90 percent certain that you are already rich. You have abundant wealth. You possess many things. Your life is more privileged than most of the people who have ever lived. You are rich.

Making you rich was not difficult. But can I make you *know* that you are rich? That is the question.

It may take a little longer, but let's see what we can do.

||||||||||||||||||||||||||||||||||||||||||||||||||||||||||||||||||||||||||||

▌Legal disclaimer

You might be thinking it's a good job I don't claim on the cover to make people rich. You could right now be planning legal action. I'd like to point out that Zondervan bears no legal responsibility for promises made on the previous page.

Anyway, you are rich. And no, you can't sue me.

"But I'm not rich," we say. "There are so many things I'd have if I were rich. Second homes, luxury cars, the best education and health care for my family, less stress and more fun!

"How can I be rich when I feel so poor?"

Now we're getting somewhere.

Are you satisfied?

One of the great consumer myths (and there are plenty to choose from) is that the market exists to create satisfied customers.

Think about it. A *truly* satisfied customer would never return to the shop!

Business depends on customers being satisfied enough to appreciate the product, but not satisfied enough to stop with just one purchase. We have to want replacement things, upgraded things or just more things.

How good is your economic theory?

At my high school I had an economics teacher from Iowa named Mr Gaulke. Mr Gaulke was a friendly, intelligent guy and a good teacher. He was also a fully paid-up market capitalist. "Merk," he would say to me (for some complicated transatlantic reason he couldn't pronounce my name properly). "Merk, man is a creature of *unlimited* needs and wants."

Technically, he was right. There is no end to any consumer's desires. So, if the right products can be offered at the right price, we will always buy and the economy will always grow. That's how the theory goes, and I learned it well. It got me my A grade but left me dry to the very depths of my soul.

Do you see this? The market is based on the idea that you will always want more. It is founded on your endless dissatisfaction. It thinks of you, as one writer, Thorstein Veblen, saw even in 1898, as a "calculator of pleasures and pains, who oscillates like a homogenous globule of desire of happiness."[1]

A globule of desire. Nice.

How does consumerism make us dissatisfied?

First, advertising creates desire. We've seen it a thousand times: enticing commercials, airbrushed models, oversized pictures of luxury foods (often glistening with water drops – why do they do that?). We watch; we want. And if we don't get, we feel that little bit poorer. A director of General Motors, Charles Kettering, once called it the organized creation of dissatisfaction.[2]

Second, there are always superior options. Supermarkets do this with food ranges: Economy or Basics, then Standard, then Finest or The Best. The net effect is that every time we don't have the most expensive option, we know there's more out there. It is tantalizingly out of reach. Sometimes there is a special offer, and the luxury option is dangled right in front of us. Maybe we get to try it once. Then the offer is over, and it is snatched away again.

Third, there's a kind of oversell that creates dissatisfaction, whether we buy or not. My favourite example of this is Lastminute.com, the ticket sales company. They promoted their travel breaks with the slogan:

Life. Book now.

Ticket sales is obviously a very competitive market, but the more I think about this, the more it stinks from every possible angle. What if I don't go on a travel break? What if I can't afford to book "life"? I guess I don't have one. That must make me, what? Dead?

But even if I do go away, this seven- to fourteen-day break is *life*. What if it rains when I get there? And when I return, what about the other fifty or so weeks of the year? Are they *non-life*?

By overselling the product, they've placed an impossible burden on it. And whether we buy or not, our daily life is made out to be dull and "life"-less.

No wonder we don't feel rich. The whole consumer machine depends on us feeling poor.

Needy

So who are the neediest people on the planet?

I guess it's us. We're the ones whose needs are constantly inflated. We're the ones who receive the majority of the world's resources (so it must be us, mustn't it?). That's why, in a recent UK survey, 60 percent of people said they didn't have enough money to buy what they "really need." Amazingly, even half of those in the highest income bracket still thought they couldn't afford what they really needed.[3]

An unbelievable transformation has taken place. As Thorsten Moritz points out:

> The needy ones are now primarily those who need instant credit to satisfy their consumerist cravings, not those who need to be provided with free grain because the last harvest was less successful than hoped for.[4]

So who's the hypnotist here? Is it me, or is it the culture we're in? What if we've been rich all along, but it just isn't in the market's interests for us to see it?

||||||||||||||||||||||||||||||||||||||||||||||||||||||||||||||||||||||||||||||||

The meaning of rich

Why be rich?

Seriously. Why would we want to carry larger wallets, employ security guards, and have more things to insure?

My guess is that it's not the beauty of the banknotes themselves; it's what being rich *means*.

To be rich is to be empowered. You can enjoy all sorts of delightful sensations. You can avoid certain kinds of suffering. To be rich is also to be privileged, with all the feelings of superiority that brings.

The logic of consumerism is that you're not rich. You aren't empowered; you can't enjoy life's finest things; you're not privileged. Not unless you pay.

But there is another logic available to us. You *are* rich. Rich in the essentials of life, and rich in its privileges too.

Would you like to know exactly how rich you are?

▌Our nonfinancial riches

In order to access our full wealth, we need to be willing to look beyond what money can measure. This isn't quite as counterintuitive as it might sound.

Who says riches have to be financial?

Who says you have to own something to enjoy it?

For instance, what is your breath worth? I mean, what would you pay to keep it? It's priceless, isn't it? But it's also free.

Money isn't nothing. It matters, and what we do with it matters. To be financially poor can be a cause of great suffering and evil. But unless we learn to think outside the pound/dollar signs, we'll never get free of consumerism.

As the saying goes, "The best things in life aren't things."

One advantage of nonfinancial riches is that they can be shared without diminishing them. A piece of music can be shared with one person, ten people, or tens of thousands. But this doesn't necessarily reduce the pleasure each person gets. It's like laughter – the more it is shared, the more it is enjoyed.

So what are these nonfinancial riches?

Let's start with life. Don't believe a word of the travel adverts. You don't have to book life; you're living it now. And to experience this most amazing, scary, wondrous journey you didn't have to pay a penny. It's a gift.

You exist. And, wait for it … you *still* exist. From second to second, you keep on existing. But why? There isn't a single scientific law to account for the fact that you are still here. You just are. And the same is true for the entire universe. All its atomic energies and chemical balances and physical principles are working now, just like they were five minutes ago, all the way back to the very beginning (which we can't explain either). We can't find a scientific reason for this. It just is.

The whole universe is one ginormous fluke of ever-increasing improbability.

Or, alternatively, it rests moment by moment on the generosity of a Giver.

Of the two possibilities, I choose option b.[5]

You exist. And you exist as "you," a unique and irreplaceable person. This is the gift of your self, your soul. There's nothing as important as this. You could accept the entire global oil revenues of the last hundred years in trade for it, and you'd be worse off. Or, as Jesus put it, "What good is it for you to gain the whole world, yet forfeit your soul?"

So life is a gift. Sometimes we can't really enjoy the gift because of pain or poverty (or, for that matter, because of busyness or selfishness). But the gift remains. And if there's one secret to receiving it well, it's learning to count our blessings from zero up rather than counting down from infinity.

Your body is part of your riches. Your capacity to touch and move and create and giggle and dance and rest. OK, my capacity to dance isn't going to make anyone rich, but you get the idea. Your nonfinancial assets receive second-by-second deposits from your five senses. For instance, what an amazing privilege it is to be able to see. Just the experience of sight itself—to have access to every kind of shape and shade, to be able to connect so clearly with the world around us. And if we have the gift of sight, isn't it incredible what we are able to wonder at?

There's the glory of nature. Life in all its bizarre and bewildering beauty. Sunrises, cloudscapes, rattlesnakes, gazelles, oak trees, teardrops, fingerprints, early morning mists, midnight stars. We don't own any of this (even if we think we own part of it, we don't). But we can enjoy it.

And we can encounter it with other people. Love is a gift (what is that worth?). Company is a gift. Community is a gift. Over the centuries we've come to benefit from wisdom to understand the world. We have culture to celebrate it. And we have language to try to express all these privileges (as far as that's possible).

Try, just try, to put a price on all of this.

Or even one bit of it.

Can you see the bottom line increasing? Can you see how rich you are?

The fact that you don't own any of the above doesn't stop it enriching your life. The fact that it's "out there" in the world and not stashed away in a private bank account makes no difference. A seventeenth-century poet, Thomas Traherne, expressed all this perfectly, using his gift of language (which is also our gift, of course, because we get to read his words):

> Your enjoyment of the World is never right, till you so esteem it, that everything in it, is more your treasure than a King's exchequer full of Gold and Silver....
>
> You never enjoy the world aright, till the Sea itself floweth in your veins,

till you are clothed with the heavens, and crowned with the stars: and perceive yourself to be the sole heir of the whole world....

Till you more feel it than your private estate, and are more present in the hemisphere, considering the glories and the beauties there, than in your own house: Till you remember how lately you were made, and how wonderful it was when you came into it: and more rejoice in the palace of your glory, than if it had been made but today morning.[6]

▌Our financial riches

I read a great book on worry once. It told the true story of a young sailor in 1926. During naval exercises, he had to set up a floating target for warships to use as nighttime firing practice. All began well. He set out with others to prepare the target. But unfortunately his forgetful comrades then sailed off without him, leaving him stranded.

So there he was, stuck in the middle of the ocean on a decoy boat, waiting to be blown out of the water by his own navy. He could do nothing all night but cling to the mast in the terrifying darkness while high-velocity shells blazed past his ears. Things were not looking great. At one point he passed out through sheer horror.

Imagine that happening to you, said the book. And then if you were worried about something in your own life, it's unlikely to seem that bad!

The naval officer survived, by the way. Every shell missed.[7]

Perspective is a powerful thing.

Our riches are not just those that all humans share. They are also, for most of us, the riches of privilege. But often we don't stand back to get a good perspective on this.

Think about ancient kings for a minute. What did they actually have?

We know they enjoyed nightly entertainment. And a few other things:

luxury bathing, fine wine (by the standards of the day), spices from around the world (if times were good) and time to reflect on the wonders of nature.

Is that so much richer than our lifestyle today?

Don't we have access to many of these privileges? Next time you've got a night to yourself, try this out. Enjoy a hot shower, crack open a bottle of Chardonnay, get in some exotic potato chips and watch a quality nature programme. And think to yourself: This is royal. I live like a monarch.

OK, they also had vast marauding armies, concubines and the tribute of nations.

But they didn't have Velcro or Pop-Tarts. You win some; you lose some.

There was once a rich young man who came to see Jesus, but left disappointed "because he had great wealth." I used to read about him and think, "Boy, he must have been rich. I'm glad I'm not that rich; otherwise it might keep me from following Jesus."

Then one day I realized: Hold on, how rich was he? Did he have hot and cold running water and round-the-clock refrigeration? Did he have advanced health care? What was the extent of his great wealth?

Camels. He had camels. Probably. And a house with several rooms (boy, that's real luxury). Maybe some fields and servants. But not the modern amenities many of us enjoy. I mean, he walked away sad; he didn't *drive* away sad!

In many ways, we are richer than him.

We are richer than most people in history, our distant ancestors, and our recent forebears. We buy about three times as much as our grandparents did at our stage of life, and about 70 percent more than our parents.

And we are richer than most people on the planet today.

> If you have food in the refrigerator, clothes on your back, a roof overhead and a place to sleep, you are richer than 75 percent of this world.

> If you have money in the bank and in your wallet or purse and spare change in a dish somewhere, you are among the top 8 percent of the world's wealthy.

> If you woke up this morning with more health than illness, you are more blessed than the million who will not survive this week.

> If you have never experienced the danger of battle, the loneliness of imprisonment, the agony of torture or the pangs of starvation, you are ahead of 500 million others who have.

> If you can read this message, you are more blessed than over two billion people in the world who cannot read at all.[8]

How do I ever forget all this?

I never used to describe myself as rich. Comfortable, maybe, but not rich. Now *rich* is exactly the adjective I would choose.

We are rich.

But this is a good thing. The richer we are, the harder we are to sell to. If we are already satisfied, we don't have to become a customer.

|||||||||||||||||||||||||||||||||||||||||||||||||||||||||||||||||||||||||||||

Overrich

I wonder if you've seen this coming.

The problem isn't that we're not rich enough; the problem is that we're *too rich.*

The riches we have are so great that they actually keep us from appreciating life in all its wonder.

How could this happen?

Riches can make us *overheated*. When I was a kid, my dad used to have this rule about not wearing coats indoors. "Aw, why not, Dad?" we would moan. But the reply was always the same: "You won't feel the benefit."

Parents are thermal geniuses. They understand that if we wear a coat indoors, our bodies acclimatize to it. The extra layer no longer makes a difference, and if we then go out in the cold, we'll be freezing. We won't feel the benefit. (Dad, if you're reading this – see, I *did* learn something!)

This applies to money.

Can money buy happiness? Yes and no. Studies show that, up to a point, money does increase happiness because it can lift people out of the harsh realities of poverty. Anyone who struggles to eat is going to be happier to have more money. However, after a certain point, having more money doesn't tend to make us any happier. Once we have food, shelter and other basics, the key to greater well-being lies elsewhere.[9]

We passed that point decades ago.

But we've adjusted to the greater comfort now. It's like we've grown used to wearing three sweaters and two coats indoors with the central heating on. Extra layers don't really help us, but it also feels impossible to give any of them up. We can't feel the benefit.

The Dalai Lama, who I imagine knows a thing or two about this, put his finger on it:

> It is fascinating. In the West, you have bigger homes, yet smaller families; you have endless conveniences – yet you never seem to have any time. You can travel anywhere in the world, yet you don't bother to cross the road to

meet your neighbours; you have more food than you could possibly eat, yet that makes people like [the overweight] miserable....

I don't think people have become more selfish, but their lives have become easier and that has spoilt them. They have less resilience, they expect more, they constantly compare themselves to others and they have too much choice – which brings no real freedom.[10]

Riches can make us *overloaded* too. I wrote a poem about this once:

If thou art rich, thou'rt poor;
For, like an ass whose back with ingots bows,
Thy bear'st thy heavy riches but a journey,
And death unloads thee.

OK, it was Shakespeare.[11] Who else says "thou'rt"? Anyway, his point was that it's better to live simply than to be a rich-ass (which is like a dumb-ass, only wealthier)! You tell 'em, Shakespeare. With every bit of extra wealth comes a greater burden. All that worry, all that time spent reading instruction booklets, all those padlocks and alarms.

It is human nature to become attached to our possessions. But as our fists clench around our property, they grow gnarled and insensitive. As Robert Kaplan said, "The more possessions one has, the more compromises one will make to protect them."[12] We become guilty and defensive about what we have. And so we have less and less time or space for the cries of the materially poor.

This is the most tragic irony of all, because contact with those who are truly needy would give us the very thing we need most: perspective.

Finally, riches can make us *overprivileged*. Psychologist Barry Schwartz points out that modern consumers have too much choice (if you can imagine such a thing).[13] He's right. When we have thousands of options from thousands of companies, a funny thing happens. The process of choosing becomes confusing and time-consuming. And the final purchase (the one-in-a-million choice) becomes so overhyped that it can't possibly fulfil our expectations. In the end, whatever extra benefit we might have got from having so many options is lost.

And anyway, what if I'd chosen the *other* one? Would I be happier ...?

All the time, while most of us wealthy consumers have too much choice, the world's poor have too little choice.

We're not just rich—we're overrich. Could it be that some redistribution of wealth would actually make life better for all of us?

▌Thanks

Would you like to start a revolutionary fightback against the worst excesses of consumerism?

Are you willing to take a bold step that will cause the house of cards to fall?

OK, then, here's what we can do. Say grace.

Before meals, we can stop. And say from the bottom of our hearts, "Thanks." This simple, regular habit carries within it the seeds to utterly transform consumerism.

Whenever I doubt the power of thankfulness, I remind myself of this reflection from the writer Rhidian Brook, after he had spent a month living in rural Kenya:

> Living in a community with a high prevalence of HIV/AIDS, a water shortage, no electricity, unreliable food, and exceptionally bad roads has seriously challenged our understanding about the world. We can't help feeling that if we'd done this earlier, we might have learned things that years of pursuing culture and pleasure have failed to teach us....
>
> You realize that your horizons have been utterly limited until now, and that these people you characterized as poor and sick and somehow lacking in

the basics are, despite all they face, talented, funny, and generous; that they live with exceptional hope and resilience, and in communities so interdependent that it makes our individualistic, self-sufficient lives seem deleterious. For a while, your whole system for measuring "wealth" gets turned upside down....

And you sit down exhausted from the roller coaster of an African day, when your seventy-year-old neighbour comes to check that you are OK (as if you are the one who is deprived), and you offer her a glass of water and she pauses before drinking and you wonder if you've broken some social protocol and then you see that she is actually thanking God for the glass of the water and for the gift of life, and you realize that all your wealth, travel, education, and privilege have never really taught you the true worth of a glass of water or been able to demonstrate how precious life is as simply and powerfully as this.[14]

Thanksgiving is powerful. However much we have, or don't have, it is the gateway to a richer life. In a society desensitized by abundance, it resensitizes us to all the privileges we enjoy.

This is what saves grace from being an empty ritual. Grace means "gift." To say grace is to remember that all life is a gift. It reminds us that though we might have prepared our food, or even grown it, we didn't create it. Though we might have paid for it, the fact that we can enjoy it today rests on factors way beyond our control.

Grace reminds us how rich we are. And if you're only as rich as you feel, then grace makes us rich.

All that, just by saying thank you.

It helps, though, if someone's listening. A wonderful, bubbly woman named Jane walked into our church last year. When I asked her how she came to faith, she described how for twenty years God had been gradually drawing her to him. She put it like this: "There were so many beautiful things in my life. And in the world too. I always wanted to say thank you. But I never knew who to say thank you to. Now I do."

This is how we'll beat consumerism – with the power of thankfulness; with intoxicating joy; with uncontainable delight. By drinking water like it's wine. By being too busy savouring life's other gifts to want another pair of shoes. By having less stuff but enjoying it more.

> *Why is everyone hungry for more? "More, more," they say.*
> *"More, more."*
> *I have God's more-than-enough,*
> *More joy in one ordinary day*
> *Than they get in all their shopping sprees.*
> *At day's end I'm ready for sound sleep,*
> *For you, GOD, have put my life back together.*
> Psalm 4:6–8 MSG

This is how we'll show that retail therapy belongs with leech therapy.

Because we are already rich.

And half the time we don't need new things; we just need new eyes.

CHAPTER 4

▌We Can Decode the System

Suppose someone wanted to change the shape of your life.

Let's say they wanted to influence what you do with your money, your time and your imagination.

How successful do you think they could be?

I guess it depends on how great their resources are.

If they had one weekend, a little bit of money and a crash course in psychology, there's probably a limit to the effect they'd have. But what if they had a budget of millions, daily access to what you see and hear from childhood and an army of marketers?

In 2008, companies in the United States and Western Europe spent around $537,000,000,000 on advertising and marketing.[1]

That's 537,000,000,000 reasons to think that advertising can have a significant influence on us. But even if *we're* not convinced, it doesn't matter. These massive budgets show that, regardless of what we believe, the corporations know that advertising is powerful. Otherwise they wouldn't spend on it like they do. Commercials may speak the language of consumer choice where the customer is king. But advertisers quietly boast to their clients that they can increase market share. It's their job.

The big money at stake also reminds us what we're dealing with. The largest 200 corporations in the world are bigger than the combined economies of every nation in the world, except the largest ten countries.[2]

This isn't just a few big companies; this is a system of huge institutions, with overlapping agendas and significant political leverage.

Systems this large tend to take on a life of their own. They exert global influence. They protect vested interests. They squeeze out alternative voices. Basically, they take on the characteristics of an empire.

This doesn't mean there aren't good people working in the system at every level (there are). It doesn't mean that the companies can't or don't bring benefits. It's just the way power works in a broken world. Whoever is most influential needs to stay on top. So, whether they intend to or not, they can end up using the tools of empire.

The Roman Empire, for instance, ruled over 5,000,000 square kilometres for more than four hundred years. Military might may have extended its borders, but that's not the only way they stayed in control. Roman power was also sustained in all sorts of other ways: commerce, coercion, seduction, distraction and threats. The consumer empire we live in is similar.

The point here is not to escape into a paranoid world of corporate baddies and noble rebels. The point is to notice what is happening so that we don't just get swept along with it.

If we're going to decode the system, this is where we have to start.

We're going to look at eight of the most common techniques at work in the consumer world.

▍#1 The deal

The other day, I popped out to the shops to rent a film for the kids.

I came back having bought three DVDs, a bottle of wine and five bags of chocolate. How did this happen?

To be honest, I'm not entirely sure. The lights were bright. The carefree music felt good. The packaging grabbed my attention. Then, the killer punch: two for the price of one.

So I bought three.

I think the buzz of getting one DVD for "free" made me feel I was on a roll. So I bought another one. That's how it is with special offers. They're like bookmakers – we feel that if we stay ahead of the game, we can make a profit at their expense. Of course, the reason they're still in business is that we don't.

The single goal of any store is to seal *the deal*. As one retail consultant put it, "Shoppers need to be somehow transformed – 'converted' – into buyers."[3] With this in mind, almost every retail environment we enter has been finely tuned. The store layout has been specially designed: essentials at the back; knickknacks by the counter where we're stuck waiting. The designers have run their focus groups. The salespeople have practised their role plays (really, in some stores, they have!). The financial incentives have been prepared – like what's called "free credit," even though it isn't "credit"; it's debt, and it isn't nearly as "free" as choosing not to buy.

There is also the magic of sales technique:

▍Phase One: Establish Rapport
- Build emotional connection with the customer
- What triggers are driving this purchase? E.g., to get fitter, protect the kids, a confidence boost (store these up for later*)

Phase Two: Product Information

- Sell the product's features as benefits (this product is easier, quicker, better)
- Steer customer towards the higher end of their budget

Phase Three: Close the Deal

- *Now* pull the emotional triggers* ("this one will definitely get you fitter/keep the kids safe/pep up your confidence")
- Preempt the sale (walk to the till, offer a pen to sign, etc.)

Phase Four: Add-ons

- Add to the sale: insurance, accessories, polish …

How many times has this been done to me? How many times have I left a store with more "bargains" than I bargained for?

My first mistake the other day was to assume that I was shopping alone. It's closer to the truth to say that at every point I was accompanied by a huge entourage of designers, behavioural psychologists and sales experts. I couldn't see them, but their work was all around me, directing my whole shopping trip towards greater consumption.

I didn't stand a chance.

#2 The promise

When is a car not a car?

When it's an adventurous dream machine, of course.

Car ads are a perfect example of *the promise*. They have only a few seconds to mark out one model from hundreds of others and to persuade us to consider parting with a significant sum of money.

"This car is like the other ones, only a different shape" isn't going to cut it.

"This car is great and has a sunroof" won't do the job either.

So what they offer is a concept, a feel, a value. Honda offers "the power of dreams." A Chevrolet convertible promises "an American revolution." A Fiat hatchback is "engineered to entertain." This is not a car; this is fantasy, this is revolution, this is fun.

It goes way beyond words. It's about establishing an association, a link in our minds. You can do this with anything: a stunning location, an evocative sound track, the face of a celebrity. Whatever it is, the association works as a promise: when you buy the product, *you somehow buy into all the rest as well.*

The promise is subtle. To explain how it works sounds clunky and ridiculous. But that's the trick. It is never explained. It is whispered, insinuated. An Oscar-winning actress just happens to be on a Chanel poster. A pro golfer just happens to wear a TAG Heuer watch. Work it out for yourself. Better still, don't work it out. Just notice. The deep wiring in our brains will make the link. Millions of dollars have changed hands to make sure that it does.

So what promises are out there?

There's *the promise of beauty.* As Germaine Greer said, "Every survey ever held has shown that the image of an attractive woman is the most effective advertising gimmick."[4] We know how it works:

The BEAUTIFUL FROCK

© 2009 Edward Monkton

"Buy me, Lady," said the frock, "and I will make you into a BEAUTIFUL and WHOLE and COMPLETE Human Being."
"Do not be SILLY," said the Man, "for a frock alone cannot do that."
"TRUE," said the Lady. "I will have the Shoes and the Bag as well."

How did we ever split the atom if we still accept logic like this? But we do.

There's *the promise of purity*. Antibacterial, pure, natural, innocent, organic, wholesome, ethical, mountain spring. Not necessarily bad things in themselves, but the promise is this: connect with the product; connect with the purity. Consume yourself to purity.

One handwash dispenser I used bore the words, "Wash your hands; it's time to start afresh." That's incredible – a liquid soap that can give you a new start in life. OK then. Speak, O Mighty Handwash! Set me free from the past! What should I do next? Will you always be here to help me?

The handwash falls eerily silent.

I have been deceived!

There's *the promise of fun*. Have you ever wondered why beer ads often use comedy? It's a promise. Beer = fun. Fun = beer. You do the math.

None of this is new.

Two thousand years ago, subjects of the Roman Empire used to dedicate sacrificial offerings to an ancient Greek goddess who promised victory. They believed that the financial cost of this was worth it. Somehow, if they only associated themselves with her name, the success of the goddess would rub off on them.

Her name was Nike.

Some things never change.

▌#3 The new

We are too materialistic.

Apparently.

But this can't be true. How can we be too materialistic when we are constantly throwing things away?

The truth is more complicated. The truth is that any one product becomes boring after a while. So how can consumerism keep us hooked? The key is to keep offering us more things than we could ever become bored of. By the time we're even slightly fed up with our last purchase, *the new* purchase is already on the horizon. And *the new* one always delivers more. It will be brighter, better, a new flavour, the next great thing. I can't wait. I'm getting excited just writing about it.

So consumerism isn't just about the material goods themselves; it's about getting rid of them and moving on to the next thing. In his book *Being Consumed*, William T. Cavanaugh describes it like this:

> There is pleasure in the pursuit of novelty, and the pleasure resides not so much in having as in wanting. Once we have obtained an item, it brings desire to a temporary halt, and the item loses some of its appeal. Possession kills desire; familiarity breeds contempt. That is why shopping, not buying itself, is the heart of consumerism. The consumerist spirit is a restless spirit ... because desire must be constantly kept on the move.[5]

Consumers live for desire. We live for *the new*, and the excitement it holds.

The retail cycle depends on this. There's a buzz as we purchase something, a chemical high (dopamine, if you must know). In that instant, all is well – we feel complete; no one is ahead of us in the game; we are the ones with purchasing power. But it doesn't last. The postconsumption glow quickly fades. The only way to get that feeling back is to buy again. So the cycle repeats ...

The new comes to us through always improved products. NEW is probably the most used, most attractive description of any product.

And to help the process along, there is accelerated obsolescence. Despite the promises of quality, often what we buy runs out faster, wears out quicker or needs upgrading sooner than it used to. This keeps the profit margins high and sends us back into the market for the next new thing.

The new comes to us through TV schedules. There's always a new series to get into, and when it's over, there will be another one after that. It comes to us through the changing seasons of fashion, with their constant repetitions and reinventions. The only guarantee we have is that our current wardrobe won't cut it for long. One UK clothes store captures this perfectly. Its name is simply: "Next."

Sport, too, is marked by these endlessly repeated seasons. As each new sports season begins, basically the same teams will compete for the same prizes by the same means. Few of these contests finally settle anything—each year the competitions reset to zero. But we're sucked into the drama again. Who knows this year who will win?

New games, new styles, new brands, new products, new shows. The carousel is constantly turning. So many new things, there isn't time to realize how similar they are. So many promises, we never stop to realize how few of them are fulfilled.

Like whining babies being entertained by a babysitter, we are constantly distracted by something new.

This has happened before. The Roman world kept itself occupied with a pagan view of the universe. There were tales of gods and mortals, told and retold, but with no particular end in sight. Each year, the various gods held out the prospect of renewal, and each year new sacrifices would be required in the hope of it.

The great advantage of a system like this is simple: a world without direction, a world going round in circles, is easier to rule. If history is a pointless dance of fate and fortune, what does it matter who's in charge? All that remains are the dazzling distractions along the way.

#4 The bluff

The fourth great trick of advertising is easiest to spot in male grooming products. For some inscrutable biological reason, we men are suckers for better gadgets. What if, for instance, a razor didn't have one blade, but two, or three? How about five? And a battery inside, too – that *must* be better. Such an innovation would scarcely deserve the humble name *razor*. At the very least it would be a Turbo Razor Extreme, but possibly what we're talking about here is a Complete Laser Grooming System.

We've all spotted this before. French thinker Jacques Ellul called it *the technological bluff* – the claim that just because something is automated, or more complicated, or computerized, it will make our lives better.

And maybe it will. But is it just me who remembers how compact discs were once announced as a long-lasting, scratch-proof musical revolution? Barely two decades later, how many unplayable and obsolete CDs gather dust on our shelves? And if technology always makes our lives easier, why is modern life so stressful?[6]

Another great bluff is *the smoke screen*. In 2009, a new TV commercial appeared in the UK. Chilled guitar music. Positive colours. An army of friendly staff giving cash to unsuspecting members of the public. It looked heavenly. It was advertising the Halifax bank. We are the bank that *gives you* money, it said. Five pounds a month, if you have a current account.

It was in fact a sensational bluff. Whoever heard of a bank simply giving away money? Halifax was actually one of the banks that contributed to the global financial collapse of the previous year. Far from bending over backwards to give its customers money, it was squeezing their interest rates, while providing million-pound pensions for the executives who had steered it into difficulty. The truth was a million miles from the ad. But that's why the bluff was so important. The bigger the smoke screen, the more there is to hide.

Lastly, *the branding bluff*. That is, if marketers can invest product lines with their own character and mystique, they can cultivate brand loyalty. Then we'll buy the product, even though it is more expensive. According to the advertising guru Saatchi & Saatchi, this is when the great brands like BMW, Guinness and Heinz become "lovemarks."

Lovemarks reach your heart as well as your mind, creating an intimate, emotional connection that you just can't live without. Ever.

Take a brand away and people will find a replacement. Take a Lovemark away and people will protest its absence. Lovemarks are a relationship, not a mere transaction. You don't just buy Lovemarks; you embrace them passionately. That's why you never want to let go.[7]

Please stop, Saatchi & Saatchi. You're scaring me now. I don't want an intimate, emotional connection with a bottle of ketchup.

Who does?!

It would sound ridiculous if it wasn't true. Brain scans have shown that the Coca-Cola logo can stimulate parts of the brain associated with emotion, cultural memory and self-image.[8] Top brands are already hardwired into our brains – not as brands, but as friends. Job done.

#5 The publicity web

The clever thing about consumerism isn't how we go to the shops; it's how the shops come to us. Because products, company sponsors, celebrities and the media are all connected, it becomes impossible to escape their influence.

This is *the publicity web.*

A classic example is Disney. They've increased revenues by creating a whole web of merchandised spin-off products. Once they've introduced a given Disney character, they can roll out its image on virtually anything: pencil cases, cups, snow globes, pyjamas. The possibilities are endless.

For instance, can anyone explain to me why the Disney car Lightning McQueen should feature on my son's potty training pants?

What could possibly be the link?

A rude suggestion springs to mind, but I won't mention it.

The publicity web works not only when one company spills into every part of our lives; it also works by connecting across different companies and media. For example:

Movie: Star Wars

Franchised toy: LEGO Star Wars

Video game: LEGO Star Wars

Supporting technology: Nintendo

Celebrity endorsement of Nintendo Wii: Frank Lampard (footballer)

Lampard's sports team: Chelsea Football Club

Football team sponsor: Samsung

*Samsung product: TV (on which to watch Star Wars—
the web is complete)*

Here's the genius – if you access the publicity web at any one point, you're brought into connection with all the rest of it. The film directs you to a toy, which is also a video game, linked to a sports star, whose team sponsor makes TVs, on which you can watch films and so on.

The publicity web is huge and inescapable. To disconnect from it you'd have to avoid TV, radio, the Internet, the news and the billboards on the street. Basically, you'd have to live in a cave.

All the time, *the publicity web* is making more and more connections. Hollywood stars appear in news features. Mickey Mouse turns up on a lampshade. The song from an advert becomes a ringtone. The thicker the web, the more "real" it feels, the deeper it penetrates our lives.

Like all systems of empire, it becomes impossible to imagine a different way of doing things. Everything is branded, linked, connected. So why not just go with the flow?

▌#6 The bombardment

So, you're an ancient empire with millions of unruly citizens. You can defeat their armies; you can patrol their city squares. But how do you really bring them into line?

Colonize their imagination.

The more we uncover of the Roman Empire, the more we see how they took every opportunity to publicize their greatness. They minted victory coins to show the latest conquered nation bowing before Caesar. They painted images of abundance on walls (like sheaves of wheat or bunches of grapes) to remind everyone of the prosperity of the empire. They filled public spaces with statues of the emperor and temples dedicated to Roman gods. As Brian Walsh and Sylvia Keesmaat explain:

> Images of the empire were … found on every imaginable object for private use. The symbolism of empire became part of daily furnishings, permeating

the visual landscape and therefore the imaginations of the subjects of the empire.[9]

You couldn't handle money or walk down the street without being reminded who was in control and how the system works. Day by day, you grow to accept the status quo.

This is *the bombardment.*

Bombardment is about saturation. Whatever we see most, regardless of whether it is true or not, we tend to accept as the dominant reality of our lives. Mark A. Burch illustrates why advertising is so powerful:

> It has been estimated that by the age of twenty, the average American has been exposed to nearly one million advertising messages, that he or she will spend a total of one year of his or her life watching television advertising. Two-thirds of newspaper space and 40 percent of our mail is unsolicited advertising.[10]

Bombardment is also about the power of suggestion. Whenever we watch an advert, flick through a catalogue or browse a shopping website, our imagination is working overtime. How would it feel if I had this? Which one is right for me? Even if we can't afford it or won't ever buy it, our desires are still being shaped by what we see. Vincent Miller writes:

> Make no mistake, such "practice of ads" is every bit as formative of our desires as more traditional religious disciplines and practices such as saying the rosary or sitting in meditation. Moreover, it is a practice to which we devote an immense amount of time. Rare is the religious practitioner who repeats a prayer or mantra as often in a day as the average person watches an ad.[11]

Bombardment is about susceptibility. Advertising not only hits us frequently but, often, below our radar. Blood-red sales posters shortcut our conscious mind to signal "this is important." TV shows carry product placements (in 2008 *American Idol* featured over four thousand of them).[12] The whole process is as subliminal as possible.

Advertising has a certain invisible power. TV, for example, contains many of the elements of hypnosis: a relaxed, semiconscious state, bright light, long exposure, voices we trust, suggestive cues ("don't miss our greatest sale") and so on.

I said to my wife, "I wonder if TV is hypnotic." She replied, "Of course it is! Don't you know what it's like trying to have a conversation with you when you're watching a movie?"

The bombardment is subtle and constant, but its most potent aspect is that it goes unchallenged. One ad follows another, then another and another. There isn't time to consider the messages. Often we are swept along in awed silence until the commercial break ends. Then, ten to fifteen minutes later, the whole process repeats …

#7 The threat

An assistant in an electrical store once followed up a purchase I'd made with this question: "Can I offer you peace of mind, sir?"

Amazing, I thought. I didn't know they were training sales reps in the pursuit of inner stillness.

It turns out he was just trying to sell me insurance.

It's bizarre, isn't it? For twenty minutes they tell you how wonderful, durable and efficient the product is. Then, as soon as you say you'll buy it, they start to suggest that it's going to fall apart!

Unfortunately, anyone who thinks they can sell you peace of mind doesn't know the first thing about it. Besides, I was more peaceful *before* he reminded me that the product I just bought could break any minute.

What looks like an offer is actually a threat.

Threats are a vital part of the marketing machine. There's the shot of the children riding safely in the back of the car (you wouldn't want anything to *happen* to them, would you?). There's the mobile phone ad full of happy, sociable people (this is the happy, sociable world of the mobile phone; if you don't have one, think how lonely you'll be).

In fact, the whole consumer treadmill is based on a hidden threat. If we don't keep up with what's currently acceptable, we'll stick out like a sore thumb. We have to keep moving; we have to avoid anything outdated or unfashionable. Like all treadmills – you stand still, you fall over. Zygmunt Bauman explains how this works in the case of old makeup:

> Beige makeup, last season a sign of boldness, is now not just a colour going out of fashion, but a dull and ugly colour, and moreover a shameful stigma ... the act which not that long ago used to signal rebellion, daring and "staying ahead of the style pack" rapidly [turns] into a symptom of sloth or cowardice ... a sign of falling behind ...[13]

The lesson is clear – leave out the beige makeup! Or maybe the lesson is that our consumer habits are driven by the anxiety of falling behind and being excluded. No wonder Lily Allen called her 2008 song about consumerism "The Fear."

The biblical book of Revelation imagined a "beast" (a ruling power – most likely the Romans) that seeks to oppress the people of God. One of the ploys used by the beast is economic blackmail. Unless God's people give in to the system, they won't be able to buy or sell.[14] It's a threat: play ball, or else. The oldest tricks are the best.

#8 The double bluff

OK, what if all this is true? What if these tricks and techniques are used on us every day of the week?

But what if the public become savvy to them? What can advertisers do then?

Answer: the double bluff.

Instead of hiding the false promises and dubious motivations, they trumpet them. It's classic reverse psychology. The bolder, the more blatant the claim, the better. The department store Selfridges led campaigns with these ads:

BUY ME – I'LL CHANGE YOUR LIFE

I shop therefore I am

The claim is so outrageous, we laugh knowingly. It's cool irony, of course. They don't really mean it; we don't really believe it. And yet a look through our bank statements might tell a different story.

The absolute master of this is the French telecom company Orange. A series of movie ads portrayed the Orange executives as a bunch of soulless, grasping idiots, determined to squeeze mobile phones into every aspect of the films they sponsor.

This is genius. Deep down, we suspect that mobile phone companies are only after our money. So the ad says, "Yes – imagine how funny it would be if we were only after your money. Imagine us as hapless profiteers. But of course we're not."

But, of course, they *are* profiteers. Ask their shareholders. It's a double bluff. This is getting really clever now. So clever that it's easier to simply play along and laugh at the insanity of it all. And laugh with Orange, which gets the joke too.

So if they get the joke, we must be able to trust them.

Right?

|||||||||||||||||||||||||||||||||||||||||||||||||||||||||||||||||||||||||||||||

What do we do now?

However we got here, there's a multibillion dollar global business dedicated to making us less satisfied, give less away and spend more than we otherwise would.

What have we got in reply?

The system can feel overwhelming. But actually it makes a big difference just to see it. We need a *Matrix* moment.

The Matrix movie is about a fake, computer-generated world that humans have become trapped in. What keeps them from escaping? The fake world is reassuringly comfortable, and they find it impossible to imagine anything different. But there is a reality outside the system. And there are some, like the main character Neo, who live inside the system but begin to realize how it all works.

At the end of the first movie, Neo reaches a new level of clarity about the system he's in. In that instant he starts to *see* the Matrix. From then on, there is no turning back. The film ends as he says:

I know you're out there. I can feel you now. I know that you're afraid. You're afraid of us. You're afraid of change. I don't know the future. I didn't come here to tell you how this is going to end. I came here to tell you how it's going to begin. I'm going to hang up this phone, and then I'm going to show these people what you don't want them to see …[15]

Once we can decode the system, a new set of choices opens up. We don't have to make *the deal*. We don't have to believe *the promise*. We don't have to pursue *the new* or accept *the bluff*. We can see through *the publicity web* and *the bombardment*. We're not as vulnerable to *the threat* or *the double bluff*.

Once we've seen how it works, the system doesn't have to rule us anymore.

▌Outshining empire

If we're going to break the power of the marketing machine, we need a model for resisting empire. We need wisdom from groups that have survived the mightiest empires without getting crushed or selling their soul. And if that's what we're looking for we may need to be prepared to be surprised, because a good contender is ...

The church.

For all its imperfections and compromises (and there are many), the church is still one of the best examples of how to resist and even transform an empire. And the first time they did it was – you guessed it – with the Romans.

Beginning in AD 30 with the execution of their founder by Roman soldiers, the early church spread through the major cities of the empire. Over the next three centuries the Christian faith proved resistant to all kinds of financial counterincentive, imperial propaganda and military threat. It was, at its very heart, empire-proof. By the early fourth century, the emperors had to come to terms with Christianity.[16]

The early church were an imperfect bunch. But the empire couldn't crush them. As a result, Western civilization was never the same again.

How did they do it?

They refused to buy into the empire's dreams. Roman soldiers were in their streets and Caesar's head was on their coins, but their hearts were elsewhere. They saw through the whole thing. And so it lost its power over them.[17]

The church had a promise of their own. An offer of life that wouldn't fade. A source of purity and newness that was free. They had a vision of the future that shattered the endless repetitions of fate.

Recently, I saw how this worked in the British Museum in London. The

Roman History rooms are full of the usual images of lofty emperors and vanquished enemies. But tucked away in a few of the display cabinets you can see a different kind of image—the traces left by the early Christians. Their new movement had a new art. They didn't go for pictures of soldiers. They went for a shepherd. And he's not crushing the weak; he's carrying them on his shoulders. The Good Shepherd had replaced the mighty emperor; because even though his power was greater than the whole empire, he displayed it in service.

In the middle of a hostile world, the Christians kept their imagination safe. Or should I say they kept it wild? They dreamed different dreams about the empire of God (his kingdom), where truth and love triumph. They kept their identity—as an anti-tribe where all are welcome, no matter what their class or status.

And they picked their battles. They didn't encourage slave revolt or new modes of government. They just formed the kind of lives the empire couldn't make and cared for those the regime forgot. As a result, they didn't just outlast empire; they outshone it. Sociologist Rodney Stark puts it like this:

> The truly revolutionary aspect of Christianity lay in moral imperatives such as *"Love one's neighbor as oneself"* … These were not just slogans. Members did nurse the sick, even during epidemics; they did support orphans, widows, the elderly, and the poor; they did concern themselves with the lot of slaves. In short, Christians created "a miniature welfare state in an empire which for the most part lacked social services." It was these *responses* to the long-standing misery of life in antiquity … that inspired Christian growth.[18]

Mute

The consumer empire will be outmanoeuvred in the same way.

It will be transformed when people see it, see through it and see beyond it to something much greater.

For a small step towards this, consider the mute button.

I can remember when I used to think that the mute button on a TV remote control was just another pointless gimmick. Now, though, I've come to realize that every mute button is slipped secretly into the design process by anticonsumerist angels. Only they know its true power.

I think we started to mute the commercials about the time the TV companies began boosting their volume. This crucial overreach pushed me to react, and in one simple move I experienced a surprising liberation.

With the sound down, the adverts lost their potency. Once-sublime celebrity endorsements became comedy charades. Without the voiceover, I couldn't tell what the medical adverts were telling me to be afraid of. Without the sound track, the tricks were easier to decode. Even better, with the sound down, Ailsa and I could talk again. And, if we chose, we could dissect what we were watching.

This one step turned us from passive consumers to critical viewers.

This is how we can resist empire:

Turn down

Tune out

Laugh

Scrutinize

Discuss

Dispute

Refuse

Reimagine

We can call the bluff of the desire creators. We don't have to give them our imaginations to fill. We don't have to let them dream our dreams for us.

We can dial out of the consumer dream and connect to a different story. A story about values the system can't control. A story that promotes not revolutionary rage but a love that infects and transforms the system, renewing it from within.

That's how the system will meet its match.

CHAPTER 5

I Will Not Maximize My Life

Have you ever watched Frank Capra's *It's a Wonderful Life*? Apparently it's one of the 100 Films to Watch Before You Die.

How about swimming with dolphins? That often tops the Things to Do Before You Die list.

Then there's 1,000 Places to See Before You Die. 100 Novels to Read Before You Die. There's even 100 Belgian Beers to Try Before You Die. And so on.

All these things to do before we die. We're going to be busy. And what about those who've never had the chance? What about people whose lives are drawing to a close without being able to do some of these things?

We could start a charity to go round old people's homes and provide once-in-a-lifetime experiences while there's still time. We could take frail geriatrics up in planes and show them *It's a Wonderful Life* before pushing them out of the cargo doors for a parachute jump wearing scuba gear so that they can land directly in coral reef lagoons to swim with dolphins within sight of Disneyland.

We could call it Die Happy.

But what if cramming in Things to Do Before You Die isn't a good thing to do before we die? What if it leads to busy, self-absorbed lives where we're always worried that we might not be making the most of what we've got?

A few years ago I was invited to a wedding. But the date clashed with a commitment I'd already made to some old friends. I was really torn. How could I miss the wedding? But then, how could I let my old friends down? Maybe I should spend the whole weekend commuting between the two venues? It was about then that I realized just how stressful it can be to maximize your life. Whichever choice I made I was going to miss out. There would be fun happening somewhere, and I wouldn't be part of it. Just possibly, I would make the wrong choice and pass up an unrepeatable experience.

The whole thing got me thinking: How did we get like this? Why are we so devoted to maximizing our lives? And will it really make us happy?

IIIIIIIIIIIIIIIIIIIIIIIIIIIIIIIIIIIIIIIIIIIIIIIIIIIIIIIIIIIIIIIIIIIIIIIIIIIIIIIIIIIII

▌Maximizing

We tend to want to maximize our lives. We want the best deal for our money. We seek the greatest pleasure from the time we have. We want the maximum quality of life and relationships. Basically, we want to maximize everything.

Now where would we get an idea like this? Who could possibly benefit from a society of people trying to make their lives as full as possible?

Make the most of now (Vodafone)

Live life to the Max (Pepsi Max)

The world is full of opportunities; don't let them pass you by (British Airways)

"Carpe diem ... seize the day, make your lives extraordinary" (Mr Keating, *Dead Poets Society*)[1]

Vodafone, Pepsi, British Airways, Hollywood – that's an interesting alliance. They're keen to latch on to something so commonplace in our culture that we accept it unthinkingly. This is the deeply held belief that one life is all we have and we should get the best of it.

So how can we maximize our lives?

We can fill them with as many experiences, entertainments and adventures as possible. In films this comes across as a noble, life-affirming approach. But advertisers are equally happy with it. They know that there are plenty of companies lining up to provide us with the experiences we're after. That's why at least one "Before You Die" website is sponsored by a travel agent. *Carpe diem* is pretty much the motto of consumerism. It could be translated "buy while stocks last."

As long as we're thinking like this – that life is made meaningful only by personal experience within a limited time frame – we'll be unstoppable consumers. We'll have an infinite desire to travel to more places, consume more products, pursue more interests and make more connections. In other words, we'll be a marketer's dream.

It won't matter how many experiences we collect. It won't matter how many of the earth's resources we use up or how low we force the wages of others; it will never be enough. There'll always be more we could experience. We'll never transcend this, never mature out of it—the only limit will be the day of our death.

And *death* is the key word here. The phrase holding all the Things to Do lists together is: "Before You Die." Death is the stark reality behind the whole maximize idea, as we see in *Dead Poets Society*—the film and novel:

> "Open your text, Pitts, to page 542 and read for us the first stanza of the poem," Keating instructed ...
>
> "Yes, sir," Pitts said. He cleared his throat.
>
> > *Gather ye rosebuds while ye may,*
> > *Old time is still a-flying:*
> > *And this same flower that smiles today,*
> > *Tomorrow will be dying.*
>
> He stopped. "Gather ye rosebuds while ye may," Keating repeated. "The Latin term for that sentiment is *carpe diem*. Does anyone know what that means?"
>
> "*Carpe diem*," Meeks, the Latin scholar, said. "Seize the day."
>
> "Very good, Mr ...?"
>
> "Meeks."
>
> "Seize the day," Keating repeated. "Why does the poet write these lines?"
>
> "Because he's in a hurry?" one student called out as the others snickered.
>
> "No, No, No! It's because we're food for worms, lads!" Keating shouted. "Because we're only going to experience a limited number of springs, summers, and falls.

"One day, hard as it is to believe, each and every one of us is going to stop breathing, turn cold, and die!"[2]

We are food for worms.

That's what this is about. It's not just about life being short (the Bible makes that point in several places); it's about this life being all there is. There's no greater hope to live for. There's no ultimate meaning, except the meaning you make for yourself. There's no verdict from a larger perspective that will make our choices worthwhile.

This could be right, of course.

There could be no God.

In that case, we probably *should* maximize our lives. Each of us can choose whatever gives meaning to our numbered days. And in the meantime the consumer carousel can be a welcome distraction from the nothingness that awaits us. Psychologists have a name for this kind of behaviour: terror management.[3]

But what we really ought to be clear about is this: trying to maximize our lives is totally bound up with this mentality. At first, it sounded like joyful openness to the significance of life. Seize the day – how life affirming! But it turns out to be driven by the certain awareness of death – which is, erm … less life affirming.

What seemed to be about life is really about death. It's like finding out that a bungee-jumping company is a subsidiary of an undertaker.

This is important. Some of us truly believe the universe is meaningless, but we need to realize how easily this leads to a lifestyle of unlimited consumption. Some of us, however, *don't* believe the universe is meaningless, but we live as if we do. We're trying to cram our lives as full as possible, constantly aware that we only have so much time left. The only honest name for this is practical atheism.

So, a maximized life is easily drawn into the consumer flow. It is dominated by the shadow of death. And it has only one reference point: me. Depending on the size of your ego, this may not seem like a big drawback. But the implications are actually huge. In 2009, The Good Childhood Report analysed the state of children's lives in the UK. Despite many positive features, it found that childhood was being blighted by family breakup, teenage unkindness and commercial pressures. And what was a significant cause of these problems?

Most of the obstacles children face today are linked to the belief that the prime duty of the individual is to make the most of her own life, rather than contribute to the good of others.[4]

Can we really afford the cost of a maximized life?

▌Limiting

I asked a group of Christians about this once:

Christianity is about getting the most out of life. True or false?

Most people went for true. They hadn't worked out how much I love trick questions. Maybe they were also thinking that it's bad to waste God's gifts, that Christianity enhances life, that kind of thing. But actually, it's not the case.

Generally speaking, the Bible isn't about getting the most out of anything. In fact, it is full of *limits*. It places many things out-of-bounds: stealing, murder and envy, for starters. When God's people wandered through the wilderness, they were told only to gather food for one day at a time. No more. Later, as farmers in the Promised Land, they were instructed to deliberately leave the edges of their fields unharvested. Why? So the poor wouldn't be left with nothing.

Don't pursue whatever you want; don't collect more than each day requires; don't maximize your harvest. Why not? Because there's a bigger picture than your individual fulfilment. Because there's a God who will somehow make sure that there's enough. That's why maximizing our lives is practical atheism.

We tend to think of freedom as the absence of all containment (tell that to a goldfish!). We tend to think our happiness increases the more we keep our options open. But that can't be right.

For many people, what's the happiest day of their life?

A wedding.

What happens to your options at a wedding?

You limit them.

At a wedding you say to someone, "I choose *you*. I choose to stick with *you*." Otherwise the vows wouldn't sound quite so romantic ("to have and to hold … unless I get interest from a supermodel").

At a wedding you limit your options to one. You embrace limitation. But through that decision a whole world of faithful love opens up.

This is actually the way God longs to relate to people. Throughout history he can't seem to last five minutes without making a covenant – a binding agreement – with someone. Noah gets a covenant, along with all living creatures (that's a lot of paperwork). Abraham and Sarah get a covenant. So do Moses and all Israel. So does Aaron. Even Phinehas gets a covenant (Who? Exactly!). That's a lot of covenant making. God seems to take delight in the power released by saying, "I choose *you*." There's even a special Hebrew name for it: *hesed* – covenant love. It has been described as love that is absolutely committed to the point of destruction.

Is this not mind-blowing? God – The Limitless One – freely accepts limits. The God for whom everything is possible makes choices and sticks by them. As with a marriage, God embraces limitation because of love. Because of you. And just like a wedding, he does it with joy.

Like most things about God, we see this play out in the life of Jesus. He could have been a maximizer. He could have pulled the big crowds, wowed the public, recruited the best, concentrated on the centres of power. But he had a very different strategy.

Jesus limited his options (not by marriage, but by singleness). He didn't travel far. He based himself in an obscure provincial outpost. He never saw Rome; he never took in the wonders of the ancient world (he didn't need to "see the world" to see the world). Twelve close followers were enough to start with, and not the sharpest tools in the box either.

But somehow this one life was rich and true and full enough to change all history.

His life was caught up in a bigger purpose, way beyond his own self-gratification. And for that cause he willingly endured the severe constriction of a Roman cross. He limited himself; he emptied himself; he let all other opportunities pass him by. But still he thought it was worth it.

Maybe he didn't believe he was food for worms.

Maybe he was right …

Life to the full?

If there's one quote from Jesus that Christians are tempted to turn into a consumer slogan, it's this: life to the full. Didn't Jesus say, "I have come that they may have life, and have it to the full"? The connection with the consumer dream is obvious. You want to maximize your life? Jesus came to make it happen!

Alarm bells should start ringing, though, when Jesus and the advertisers say the same thing. Actually, Jesus saying "Maximize your life" would have been as likely as him ordering a ham and pineapple pizza for the Last Supper. But because we're so conditioned to maximize our lives, we naturally hear Jesus' words that way. We easily imagine a bigger bubble of possessions, a greater collection of experiences. We confuse "life to the full" with a full life.

But that's not what life to the full means.[5] Jesus isn't offering a course in self-advancement or a cure for baldness.

The life Jesus talks about in John's gospel is to know God, to escape the tragic consequences of sin, and to be raised to a new existence after death (if that doesn't sound like life to the full, we've got the consumer bug worse than we think).

I'm not suggesting that by *life* Jesus meant some kind of distant dream. Right now, the life he offers really is LIFE, a new way of living (and dying). But it has nothing to do with collecting more and more stuff. Quite the opposite.

The Greek word in John 10:10 often translated "to the full" is *perissos*. It means "abundantly," but also "more than enough" or "with some to spare." In the Bible, *perissos* describes the money we have left over to give to charity. *Perissos* is the food we don't need because we've had plenty. It's the name for the baskets of spare crumbs gathered up after the hungry have been fed.[6]

Words in the *perissos* family are sometimes translated as "overflow." Paul uses them to explain how God's gift to us in Jesus Christ *overflows* to many people in need of grace. He also uses them to describe the way poor Christians in Macedonia let sacrificial giving *overflow* through them, even though they basically had nothing left.[7]

In other words, this is not about the consumer dream. When *perissos* applies to possessions in the Bible, it doesn't mean life to the full.

It means *life to the overflow.*

Life to the overflow is about having above and beyond what we need *so that we can share.*

It's about living with less so that others might be blessed.

It's not about having; it's about giving.

Life to the overflow isn't an ever-increasing bubble of possessions; it's more like a cup that, when it is filled up, spills over into the lives of others.

That's very different from maximizing your life.

Apples

Is life finite?

Will it run out on us?

The answer to that question makes a significant difference.

Imagine, for instance, buying a bag of apples.

The apples are yours—you bought them and you can do what you want with them. Until they go bad, that is. We can preserve and shrink-wrap apples as much as we like, but one day they will rot. The apples are a *finite resource*.

The only thing you can do is maximize your enjoyment. You can eat the apples while you have them, but you know that every bite brings you closer to the end.

This is the way some people approach life. You have only one life. You can do with it what you like, but soon (who knows exactly when?) it will be over. Make the best of it.

This approach is unlikely to lead to much sharing. There's only so much to go round, and time is short. It's more likely to lead to rushing around, consuming what we can. But even when we do consume, the pleasure will be tainted. Everything is over too soon. This might be as good as it gets.

But what if it was different?

What if life isn't a finite resource?

What if, instead, it's a gift that promises more?

Here comes the paradigm shift.

Imagine someone gives you an apple tree.

The apples are yours, but not in the same way. They are a gift. And they won't run out. No matter how nice each apple is, there will always be more to come (so there's plenty to share too). Every bite of these apples promises more.

This is a different way to live.

People with this approach to life don't feel the same sense of entitlement. Everything they have is a gift to be thankful for and to share. There's not the same rush to squeeze the best out of everything. Life doesn't narrow down to a point of despair; it opens up to a horizon of hope.

The best way to stop maximizing our lives is to have this kind of gift mentality.

Basically, we need someone to give us an apple tree. So to speak. We need life to be *a gift that promises more*. If it is, then we are free. If it isn't, then we are left with the trolley-dash philosophy of a meaningless universe.

Something within all of us longs for more than this. We yearn after life's goodness in a way that suggests there is more out there. We feel, deep down, that the beauty and love and truth in the world is more than an evolutionary trick to preserve our genes. We suspect, and desperately hope, that life is more than a finite resource. But how do we know this isn't wishful thinking?

Harry Williams, the Cambridge theologian, got this just right:

> It is natural for us to always want more – more love, more money, more prestige, more everything.... But our wanting more in fact goes deeper than anything that our earthly environment can supply, and we misunderstand it if we imagine it can finally be appeased by what this limited world can give us. For our desire is literally insatiable, which means that it belongs to the order of infinity. Our always wanting more is the way in which we clumsily express our intuition that we were made for what is endless and without bounds, that is, for God.[8]

Triple enjoyment

Forgive me if I get a bit excited. This is the point where Christianity comes alive.

For the Christian, every good thing is a gift.

First of all, it's a gift because it springs from a Source far beyond us. All that we have is a personal, ongoing, loving gift from God: "He himself gives everyone life and breath and everything else."[9] Every moment, the good things in our lives whisper to us that God is there and he is good.

Even quite simple things are transformed by being a gift. This is illustrated by The First Law of Someone Else's Chocolates. Do you ever notice how when someone else has chocolates, those chocolates always seem particularly desirable? And if they offer you one, it tastes great. But when you traipse down to the shops to buy some chocolates for yourself, they never taste quite as nice. Why not? For the same reason we don't buy ourselves greeting cards. It's the *giving* that makes it special.

Everything is a gift for a second reason, though. Despite the lavish generosity of God, we humans have a species-long habit of turning our lives in on themselves. We default on the goodness of God and seem unable to prise ourselves away from the centre of the universe. Because of this, by rights we forfeit everything. So actually, there's not a single thing we deserve.

But God is more generous still. What we forfeit, he gives back to us. He took the cost of our selfishness onto himself on the cross. Now we, the undeserving, can receive once again what we have no earthly right to enjoy.

This changes everything. Every breath I take, I don't deserve. Each day, I receive my life back again, as from the dead. The new light of the dawn is doubly sweet – "his compassions … are new every morning."[10] All that I have, God hasn't just given me once, but twice.

There is one more reason that everything is a gift. For those who love God, every good thing is a promise, a sign of what is to come. When you savour the sweetness of rain, or the brooding darkness of thunder, or the first lick of an ice cream on a sweltering summer's day, you don't just enjoy the thing itself; you can also enjoy the fact that whatever is coming next will be brighter, greater, more intense and no longer subject to decay. Like watching a movie trailer, you can enjoy both the present experience and the anticipation of what's to come *at the same time*.

God is preparing a new creation for anyone who would like to join it. The passage of time isn't cause for despair; it's reason for hope. The more time passes, the closer we get to the grand event.[11]

So Christians should enjoy everything three times: once as a gift we didn't create, once as a privilege we don't deserve and once as a promise we're yet to receive. Triple enjoyment, not constant cramming, is the key.

Of course, the gift mentality isn't unique to Christian teaching. There are lifestyle gurus who associate it with living as a child of the universe. There are business experts who recommend a win-win mentality, where there is somehow enough for everyone. But none of them have a reason *why*.

No one seems able to explain why, in our finite lives, we should trust the infinite.

But Christianity has a reason. The infinite God is passionately involved in his world. He created and sustains it. He entered into history to redeem it through a life of flesh and blood. And he gave his promise of new creation when Jesus rose from the dead and appeared to eyewitnesses.

So life really is a gift. There really is an abundance. Our lives don't have to be defined by the shadow of death. This is why we can leave maximizing behind for good.

Going to Greece

I saw a great ad the other day:

You only live once: Holiday in Denmark
—Danish Tourist Board

I admit I did a double take. I started wondering—even if I *did* believe that I'll only live once, would that actually motivate me to go on holiday in Denmark? I mean, Denmark? Maybe if I lived one hundred times …

Maybe not even then.

Greece, however, is another matter. The Greek coastline with its translucent sapphire waters and platinum pure beaches. The Acropolis of Athens. The sunshine. The Greekness.

If you live only once, go to Greece.

But what if you don't live only once?

What if you've been promised that you'll live again?

Then Greece would be nice, but you don't *have* to go. You're free. Free to go. Free not to go. Free to invest in the place and time in which you find yourself. Free to use your money for something else, if you choose.

Me personally, I've been close, but I've never explored the Greek mainland. I'd love to, though, and maybe one day I will. But seeing as Jesus promises the renewal of all things at the new creation, I'm pretty confident that whatever's best about Greece will somehow be there.

So I have concrete plans to see Greece.

Just not yet.

▌Life within limits

This is the alternative to a maxed-out life. This is the final key to consumer breakout. Instead of trying to maximize our lives, we are free to live within limits.

This doesn't mean we won't ever travel or try anything adventurous or do anything significant. It's just that we don't have to do it all at once.

We don't have to hoover up every sensation, rate every experience, fill our passports with stamps or our albums with photos. We can experience each moment of life for what it is.

And then a strange thing will happen.

Our experience of each day actually becomes richer. Free from the burden of making it into our Top Ten, our journeys can take on a meaning all of their own. Each triple-gifted morning can bring its own new mercies. Without being constantly measured and compared, our happiness is released to take us by surprise.

Our limits don't deaden us; they help us come alive. Like lines on a sports pitch, our limits allow us to play.

I will not maximize my life.

The marketeers don't know what to do with such a person.

||||||||||||||||||||||||||||||||||||||||||||||||||||||||||||||||||||||||||||

Rhythm and soul

At the end of the day, the problem with a maximized life is that it's always ON. All systems are constantly go. A maximized life has no rhythm, and therefore no music. It has no poetry, no soul.

But life is all about rhythm.

Where did I get that idea? I guess I just looked out of the window over time and saw the seasons changing.

Rhythms are everywhere. Dawn and dusk, ebb and flow, the beating of our hearts, our very breathing. Rhythm is sewn into the fabric of life.

We ignore this at our peril. Sleep and wakefulness, harvest and replenishing, even the natural peak and trough of the chemicals in our brain. We need to respect the balance.

The rhythmless monotony of consumerism is a mark of modern life. But if we can relearn the rhythms, we can break out of the consumer crush. The next four chapters aim to do just that. Each one explores a vital rhythm.

As long as we're dead set on maximization, though, we'll have no space to catch this. We'll lose the gentle pulse of life in the white noise of rush. Only if we're willing to turn down the volume of our lives can we rediscover rhythm and, with it, soul.

This is exactly the offer that Jesus made.

> Are you tired? Worn out? Burned out on religion? Come to me. Get away with me and you'll recover your life. I'll show you how to take a real rest. Walk with me and work with me – watch how I do it. Learn the unforced rhythms of grace. I won't lay anything heavy or ill-fitting on you. Keep company with me and you'll learn to live freely and lightly.[12]

The unforced rhythms of grace. Not hyped-up religious overdrive or tightly packed life experience. Grace. It has a music all of its own.

Jesus offered a straightforward deal. Not 100 Things to Do Before You Die. Not even 10. Just one: Seek first the kingdom of God and his righteousness – everything else will be given to you as well.

Not only is this infinitely simpler than chasing endless lists; it's also something that everyone can do. No skis necessary. No batteries required. If life is all about starring in My Personal Adventure, then the healthy, the wealthy and the young will always have the upper hand. But the adventure of the kingdom is open to all comers. It places value on people more than on experiences. From the foetus who is not yet able to make life-enhancing choices, to the dying who are too late to make them, to the multitude living on a dollar a day who cannot afford to maximize their lives. Their lives are valuable not because of their experiences. They are valuable because they are part of something bigger, because they are seen and known by God.

The kingdom issues an invitation to measure our lives differently. In the words of the English poet Philip James Bailey:

> *We live in deeds, not years; in thoughts, not breaths;*
> *In feelings, not in figures on a dial.*
> *We should count time by heart-throbs. He most lives*
> *Who thinks most, feels noblest, acts the best.*[13]

If this is a kind of maximizing, it's not at all what the advertisers have in mind.

So, I'm sorry, Vodafone. I choose not to make the most of now.

Sorry, Pepsi, I will not live life to the max.

Sorry, Hollywood, I choose a different story.

I choose to look beyond personal experience.

To focus beyond the horizon of my life,

To glimpse a bigger kingdom,

To see a brighter, dawning hope that embraces everyone who seeks it.

PART TWO

Rhythms of Life

CHAPTER 6

The Power of Stop
(Create & Rest)

When I was at college, living away from my parents for the first time, I was given my own room. This was a grave error.

Without the restraining influence of my parents, mess of every kind began to envelop my room, like the slowly extending tentacles of some kind of chaos monster.

My floor became messy. My bed became messy. Occasionally I would wake up to find myself sharing a bed with unexplained things:

Particles of dirt (never sleep in shoes, folks).

Broken glass.

Once I woke up with an entire drum kit.

My timetable was messy too. I would roll out of bed three minutes before class. My essays mounted up like bad debts. As deadline day approached and went by, I would work through the night for several days in a row.

The antidote to all this was Steve. Steve was a placid, well-rounded guy I got to know early on in my first term. His room, on the opposite side of the quadrangle, was an oasis of peace. His carpet was clean. His room smelt fresh. He always had a drink on offer, and possibly chocolate cake. Basically, his life held together while mine was pretty much boundaryless.

The great indicator of this was Sunday. On Sundays, Steve – a top-grade student – would stop his work to rest, worship and generally enjoy himself. My enjoyment and rest was scattered randomly through the term. It gathered in indulgent pools, whole lazy weeks. But then when the work needed doing, I knew no rest at all. I would slave away in the lonely darkness of the early hours, facing down the demons of worry and despair.

Steve had a stillness. He had poise. And the sign of this was that once a week he could afford to stop. He had Sabbath. As Steve himself pointed out to me some years later, a stone skimming on water doesn't drop beneath the surface until it slows down. Sunday was his day to drop beneath the surface. It was his day for the power of stop.

||||||||||||||||||||||||||||||||||||||||||||||||||||||||||||||||||||||||||||||||||

24/7 life

Stop is not the world's favourite word right now. *Go* is more positive, and twice as economical with letters.

We live in the world of "always on." TV is available through the night (do you remember when it wasn't?). We can shop online round the clock. We can eat fruit in or out of season (do we even know what fruit is in season now?).

Nothing is allowed to stop us. Electric light triumphs over the restfulness of night. Caffeine conquers tiredness; aspirin vanquishes pain. The free market overcomes union objections to shift work. We can work and shop and choose anytime, all the time. Nonstop.

But 24/7 life is exhausting. The treadmill never stops. Our consumer lifestyle requires more and more income to sustain it. So we can't allow ourselves to rest (and the increasing numbers of people who work through the night for us aren't allowed to rest either). At home and at work, the ceaseless pace takes its toll.

Our lives can end up like Marcia K. Hornok's cruel parody of the 23rd Psalm:

The clock is my dictator, I shall not rest
It makes me lie down only when exhausted
It leads me to deep depression
It hounds my soul.
It leads me in circles of frenzy for activity's sake.
Even though I run frantically from task to task,
I will never get it done,
For my "ideal" is with me,
Deadlines and my need for approval, they drive me.
They demand performance from me, beyond the limits of my schedule.
They anoint my head with migraines.
My in-basket overflows.
Surely fatigue and time pressure shall follow me all the days of my life,
And I will dwell in the bonds of frustration forever.[1]

Compared with thirty years ago, we work longer and sleep less. Many of us struggle to value our jobs. They can easily become just a means to money, bankrolling our lifestyle, working in order to "live." At the same time, our leisure is overloaded. The holiday has to be good enough to justify the work that made it possible. And we rarely seem to have enough time to enjoy it.

Create and rest

We need a different rhythm.

But to find it, we need a different music. There's some available to us in the Hebrew song of creation, also known as the first chapter of the Bible. It's a kind of hymn with seven verses. I say seven verses—it's more like six verses and then a long pause.

Here's the pause:

> God saw all that he had made, and it was very good. And there was evening, and there was morning—the sixth day.
>
> Thus the heavens and the earth were completed in all their vast array.
>
> By the seventh day God had finished the work he had been doing; so on the seventh day he rested from all his work. Then God blessed the seventh day and made it holy, because on it he rested from all the work of creating that he had done.[2]

Six days to shape a nascent world. Light and life fill the emptiness; space and order subdue the chaos. He fills; he subdues. He creates; he rests. And the rest is a Sabbath.

In Hebrew, the word *sabbath* means "stop."

This is the divine rhythm: create and rest. Six days on the go; one day to stop. "And there was evening, and there was morning" indicates that he also has a break each evening. So he takes the nights off too.

I was looking at these verses with some local office workers recently, and one guy asked a fascinating question: "Why did God rest on the seventh day? It makes it sound like he's weak."

Do you ever notice how sometimes the questions we ask reveal more than the answers?

Rest = weakness. That's how it can sound to us. Like God is powerful enough to generate and sustain the energy that composes the whole universe, powerful enough to bring into being the whole panoply of speciated life, but not powerful enough to get to the end of a working week without needing to put his feet up. I'm not sure that washes.

So if Sabbath isn't a sign of weakness, what is it?

It's a sign of strength. Sometimes it takes more power to stop than it does to start (think of a forest fire). Sabbath requires composure. It requires the strength of will to interrupt the momentum of work. Enough. Now I rest.

Sabbath is a sign of joy. There's a kind of blessed delight in the way God rests. He stands back like a satisfied artist. It's good work – even if he says so himself.

Sabbath is a sign of contentment. God stops. But was everything really finished? He'd only worked for six days. OK, he'd accomplished a lot. But was everything finally completed, perfect, job done? I don't think so.

The world still needed filling and subduing. No matter. He delegated that.

Fill the earth and subdue it, he told his apprentices. That is, us.[3] He allowed us to take a level of responsibility for our world.

Maybe God is more willing to trust others than we are?

Creating and resting is essential. When Genesis 1 states, "God blessed the seventh day and made it holy," part of what it means is that he planted this pattern in the very heart of the universe. So anyone searching for life and goodness (in other words, anyone wanting to be blessed) needs to take hold of the create/rest rhythm.

Consider what happens when we don't rest. To go without sleep is torture. Literally.

For most of us it's less extreme, but for those (like me) who are driven by a restless internal engine, the effects are there all the same. Life, we come to realize, has a way of bringing us to a halt. One way or another. Workaholics can get away with it for so long. But eventually they find themselves plunging into sudden and unexpected depressions. "It's a mystery," people remark. "They seemed so full of energy and life." But it's not a mystery. Our bodies and our minds need rest – if they don't get it, they can flick into automatic standby like a computer conserving energy.

Rest has a way of finding us. One way or another.

Something like this happened to the Hebrew nation. The God who rescued them from slavery in Egypt gave them Sabbath. It was their day of joy and contentment and trust. It also served as a check on overwork. The Sabbath limited harsh slave labour, protected animals from exhaustion and safeguarded the richness of the soil.[4]

But, over the centuries, God's people forgot the rhythms of covenant and the One who gave them. They chased the gods of success and safety. They had no time for Sabbath, no time for justice. The land suffered. The workers suffered.

Then one day they had the unwelcome experience of being deported to a foreign land. At that point, the history writers add an interesting footnote:

> Nebuchadnezzar ... set fire to God's temple and broke down the wall of Jerusalem; [his army] burned all the palaces and destroyed everything of value there.

He carried into exile to Babylon the remnant, who escaped from the sword, and they became servants to him and his sons until the kingdom of Persia came to power. The land enjoyed its sabbath rests; all the time of its desolation it rested ...[5]

Tragic burnout. Their life was unsustainable. They were brought to a halt. And when they were gone, "the land enjoyed its sabbath rests." It's ironic – enjoying rest was the very thing God had asked them to do in the first place. If only they had listened.

Orbit

Q: What day is it on the sun right now?

A: It's not really any day.

Essentially, the sun knows no calendar time; it has no day or night, or weeks or years. There's only the consuming blaze of endless light. The sun sits at the centre of the system that bears its name. And it is always on.

But we are not the sun.

We need night.

We need off.

So we can't live at the centre.

The sun is impossible for humans to live on. It's just that bit too hot. And life is like this. The centre is just too intense a place for us to be. We burn out. Everything ends up circling around us, but we ourselves never rest.

This is where the power of stopping comes in. It coaxes us away from the centre of the universe. It clears time for us to remember that everything doesn't revolve around us. Norman Wirzba writes:

Sabbath observance thus gives us the time and the space to take a considered look at what our work is finally about. Our temptation is to think that we live through our own effort and that the goods we enjoy are ours because we have earned and deserve them. A moment's reflection can quickly dispel that illusion, as everywhere we look we can see the generosity of others: earthworms aerating and rebuilding soil, plants turning sunlight into energy, family providing for us since birth, teachers looking out for our children. The list of kindnesses goes on and on, but we often fail to notice. We are simply too busy with our own agendas and our sense of self-importance.[6]

When we stop, we vacate the centre. And when we do that, something truly wonderful happens: there is time for day and night. It's only when we step away from the centre that our lives assume their proper orbit, with their own day and night, activity and rest. This is the rhythm we were made for. Daytime–to live and work and learn. A time to *achieve*. Nighttime–to do nothing, to lie still and let the world go on without us. A time to *receive* rest and refreshment, while the earth turns and the new day comes of its own accord.

The truth is, though, something keeps us from stopping. Something makes it hard to leave the centre. Despite all our complaints about busyness, we like being in control of things, in touch, needed. Without this, we feel insignificant.

Besides, if I do vacate the centre, what will happen? Who will provide? Who will watch over my world? If I stop, will my best be good enough?

Only grace can break this cycle.

Only the choice to believe that we can safely vacate the centre. That place belongs to someone else. It belongs to one "like the sun." It belongs to God, who "neither slumbers nor sleeps" because he is always watching over us.[7] And if he doesn't sleep, we can. My friend Viv Thomas puts it beautifully: You can rest your head on the pillow of the Father's love, place your weight on the work of the Son, and let the Spirit carry your feet. That is true rest.

||||||||||||||||||||||||||||||||||||||||||||||||||||||||||||||||||||||||||||

Consumer lifestyle detunes the song of creation in two ways. First, instead of creating, we only consume. Second, instead of resting we never stop. To regain the first great rhythm of life, we need to relearn creation and rest.

But creating is much bigger than simply work. And rest is more than just taking a day off.

Live creatively

We were created to create, made to make. It's part of bearing the image of God, and it keeps DIY stores in business. Creativity runs in our divinely given DNA.

How can we get in touch with this?

We could begin by valuing the creativity of our daily work. You may feel your daily business is very creative. You might be Designer in Chief for The Artistic Garden Emporium; you might not. But all our work is part of the commission to fill and subdue the earth.

Think about it. How many jobs help produce healthy, happy, well-fed people? Whether it's midwifery, catering, delivering groceries or being a central-heating technician, it is part of *filling* the earth with flourishing people. It is creativity. Or your work may involve discovering, utilizing, and developing the resources of our world or passing on this knowledge. Science, engineering, education – that's *subduing* the earth. If you're involved in filling or subduing the earth, you're on divine assignment. You're exercising the delegated creativity of God!

Only a few jobs don't fit this brief. I guess you could be a Deputy Globe Emptier or Executive Chaos Implementer (actually, can you *implement* chaos?).

Just possibly your work does involve shortening people's lives or poorly stewarding the earth's resources.

If that's the case, maybe it's time for a retrain?

But for many of us, we can start by being thankful for our work and bringing to it as much diligent creativity as we can.

Another aspect of creativity is to respect created things. When we make something, we put a little bit of ourselves into the task. You can test this by destroying something a child has recently made and seeing if it bothers them. On second thoughts, maybe don't. No created thing is worthless—it reflects and celebrates its maker. That goes for the planet we live on, and it also goes for everything we buy.

So many consumer products come to us faceless, with makes but not makers, without craftsmanship or personal pride. It's easy to forget that every consumer good we purchase is part of the world God lovingly and intricately created. And they've been made by people who bear his image. That's right—even paper clips. If we forget this, we can end up treating things without respect. We use them thoughtlessly or inefficiently. We buy impulsively and let them waste away in a cupboard, or we allow ourselves to be wooed by the next thing and throw them away before they're even broken.

Remember how consumerism isn't about delighting in things but about the desire for *new* things? But when we live creatively, we respect the things we already have. We use them with gratitude and care. We love our possessions more, not less.

We can take an interest in how our things were made. Were the workers paid fairly? If animals were involved, how were they treated? If it's food, where was it grown? Was this product made in a way that values the planet? Where and how will we dispose of it? (When God said, "Fill the earth," I'm guessing he wasn't talking about landfill.)

No product is just a product. Food is not just fuel; clothes are not just fashion items; cheap goods are not just bargains. They are the work of someone's hands, and they have a value (which is not the same thing as having a price). Those who live creatively buy things they can respect and respect the things they buy.

Last of all, we can indulge in the riotous pleasures of simple creativity. Buying stuff in a packet and then throwing it away is not the pinnacle of human purpose. But when we cook or garden or compose, when we make (or when we make do), when we fix what is broken, we're fulfilling the creation mandate. Even when we find a new purpose for something or recycle it so it can be remade, we're being creative. As G. K. Chesterton said, "Thrift is poetic because it is creative; waste is unpoetic because it is waste."[8]

Making is just fun too! And it makes our stuff more precious. My favourite sofa is the one my sister-in-law Satoko covered for us. My wife's favourite meal is the one I cook for her. She just wishes I cooked it more often.

Stopping

Considering that it doesn't involve us doing much, stopping is an amazingly productive use of our time.

Stopping recharges us. It gives us the kind of rest that goes beyond leisure-crammed holiday time. It is creative but in a different way. I suppose that's why it's called re-creation.

Stopping allows us to play. Which is a good enough reason in itself.

Stopping breaks the consumer cycle. In many ways, it is the key to resisting consumerism. Whenever we stop, we call a halt on the world of catching up with others and desiring the next thing. We create some space, some order, in the consumer chaos.

They say you never know what's controlling you until you try to give it up.

Many's the person who has said, "I'm not too dependent on alcohol, but I couldn't give it up for a month."

It's when we think about stopping that we see how things really are. We realize that we can't imagine getting through the morning without coffee. Why is that? Do we need caffeine to live? ("Yes," you might say, "we do.") We realize that a weekend without a trip to the shops would be boring. Why is that? Stopping confronts us with what is going on all the time under the surface of our lives.

Stopping also brings a freedom. Once we've pushed through the pain barrier, we realize that we *can* live without these things. There's a bracing liberty on the other side of abstinence. We don't need to consume like we do. We can stop, and then we can choose where to go next. We have that dignity.

Since its early days, the church has had a rhythm of stopping each year for forty days before Easter. Lent is a season dedicated to the power of stop, to exposing the cravings that drive us and stripping the soul down to its vulnerable beauty.

OK, so it doesn't always turn out smoothly. My latest effort – giving up "sugar and sugary things" for Lent – turned out to be a bit of a nightmare. It was like giving up breathing. I was in a foul mood all day. I overcompensated with crisps and nuts, if you can call that compensation. I ended up bending the rules beyond all recognition. It's amazing what doesn't count as "sugary" if you try hard enough. After a few weeks, I basically threw in the towel before my life fell to pieces.

There's no point being legalistic. A friend of mine decided to give up swearing for Lent. I daren't think what happened on Easter Day …

Any ancient practice can turn into an empty resolution. But often the discipline of stopping allows the quiet music of rest to have its way. The power is not in our self-will; the power is hidden in the rhythm God has given us. When we allow it to work in us, we are never the same again.

Ailsa and I gave up using the car one Lent. I didn't think we were going to manage. But we did, and our mileage hasn't been the same since. Another year we cut out nonfood shopping. The effect was detoxifying. We no longer go shopping merely for entertainment, like we used to.

Last of all, stopping is about just being who we are, where we are.

When we stop, we're no longer having or buying or doing or choosing. We just are. And we realize that this doesn't kill us. For a moment, our needs drop away like scales from our eyes. And often, when we're open to it, a sense of peace settles on the interior of our life – a stillness and wonder at all the glories that surround us. This is exactly the sensation that God had on day seven. His command to rest is an invitation to share that feeling. Sabbath is a school of divine contentment.[9]

But you don't have to wait till Sunday to experience this (or Saturday, or whatever day you could take some rest).

You can stop now.

Breathe in deep; feel the oxygen rushing inside you. Exhale the strivings.

Take some time to receive life as a gift. Dwell for a moment on the fact that your life is not your creation, and every good thing in your world has been given to you.

Get off the throne at the centre of the universe and see if someone else fits it better.

Breathe.

The world says: Hurry, rush, quick, now, on demand, immediate …

Sabbath says:

Stop

Rest

The world says: Maximize, capitalize, more, greater, bigger, only one life, you must have, you can't do without ...

Sabbath says:

Stop

Rest

The enough you're chasing is never enough.

The enough you have already is.

The first and most practical thing we can do to reconnect with the rhythms of life is nothing.

CHAPTER 7

Life in High-Definition
(Presence & Absence)

So there I am, sitting in front of a brand-new TV screen, looking for *the difference*. I switch it to high-definition digital. I switch it back. HD. Non-HD. HD. Non-HD. And so on – you get the picture. Have you ever done this? Maybe you have better things to do with your time.

Anyway, it might be the TV set I was using, but I couldn't really appreciate *the difference*. I wasn't physically lifted up from my seat and plunged into the Technicolor brilliance of another world. I wasn't confronted by an image so sharp that I had to be careful not to injure myself. It looked a little different, but I didn't *feel* any different. Maybe it's me – maybe I'm not HD-compatible.

So my first experience of high-definition TV didn't live up to the publicity. Mind you, the publicity was pretty bold stuff. For example, one advert read like this:

Life's more intense in HD
Imagine being able to see every blade of grass
on the football pitch as your team hits the winning goal.

Let's just think about this for a minute. "Every blade of grass." Why would you want to see every blade of grass?

Is grass that interesting?

Does distinguishing between the blades make for a better sport-watching experience ("Hey, look at that one there!")?

Anyway, why would you want to look at the grass "as your team hits the winning goal"?

Surely if you're looking at the grass, *you'll miss the goal*!

I'm not against TV in general or HDTV in particular. Some of the best, most thought-provoking things I've ever seen have been on a TV screen. A baby growing in the womb. Dolphins leaping through ocean waves. A guy trying to skate along a handrail but falling on his face. But I do wonder if, to coin a phrase, the advertisers of HD can't see the goal for the grass. Besides, if you want to see lots of grass close-up, why not go and lie down in a field?

Maybe that idea is not as crazy as it sounds.

Technology is a funny thing. It promises life in high-definition but delivers life sat on a sofa. Good though TV can be, if we spend long periods of time in front of it, certain changes tend to take place. We walk away from the screen with a slight headache. Everything looks duller; we feel lethargic, zoned out. People are just not quite the same in real life. They're not as amenable to our dreams, not as airbrushed or talented or funny. And to make matters worse, changing company is harder than changing channels. Here's the irony – the very thing that promised us life in high-definition can make us *less able* to appreciate our daily existence.

The truly high-definition things in your life are the things that surround you right now. Whatever you're sitting on. Whatever your view is. Whoever you're with. TV, film, and the Internet can only ever approximate this. So the proper definition of HDTV is this:

High-Definition: higher-definition than the older type of TV, but still nowhere near as high-definition as anything you're actually looking at.

In fact, the screens we look at are just about the only nonhigh-definition thing in our lives. Everything else is 3-D, full colour, natural, high-definition, surround sound. Or real, for short. So why settle for less?

▌ Two modes

High-definition is about sharpness. It's about seeing clearly, paying a special kind of attention. But this has much more to do with our attitude to what's around us than with the technology in our living room. The high-definition world that surrounds us each day is alive with innumerable delights, puzzles, and sensations. It bristles with wonder like static. In the words of a poet, "The world is charged with the grandeur of God."[1]

How can we encounter this amazing reality?

There are two modes of being in life: we're either with others, or we're not (rocket science, I know, but bear with it). If we're going to catch the wonders of life, we need to learn the rhythm of presence and absence:

Presence: being alert to those around us, alive to what they are saying, and attentive to their needs

Absence: withdrawing from others for quiet and stillness

If these are two essential ways of walking through life, you'll quickly notice that we struggle to do either of them properly. For many of us, when we're with others, we're not 100 percent with them. Our presence is watered-down by us being preoccupied, rushed or interrupted. And when we're on our own, we're not 100 percent absent—we make sure that we're contactable or busy, or we just keep ourselves amused. Our constantly connected life grants us a bittersweet privilege: we can be reached by others everywhere, but as a result we're never fully present anywhere.

Truth be told, I'm tired of living a distracted life. I'm fed up of playing with my kids but really planning next Sunday's talk. I know that I wasn't made to be talking to one person while looking over their shoulder for someone else. I'm looking for a different way of being.

How about it?

▌Distracted from presence

There's a city law boss, known to a friend of mine, who likes to be kept in touch with developments in his firm. He has a BlackBerry, and he keeps it with him. Nothing wrong with that, you might be thinking. One night, though, he was at home making love to his wife. All of a sudden, the BlackBerry rings. It's one of those difficult choices – sex or phone call? Intimate physical pleasure giving with the woman of your life, or speak to Martin from Accounts. So what did he choose? He chose the BlackBerry. But as it turns out, this wasn't too inconvenient. He had kept it on his pillow the whole time!

Call me a hopeless romantic, but I wonder if having a BlackBerry on your pillow during sex is a failure to be fully present to the other person.

When it comes to distracting us from others, there's nothing quite like a mobile phone. Mobile phones are able to say, in a unique way, "I'm with you, but I'm not with you." It could be as blunt as, "I'm in your presence, but I'm not listening to you at all." Or it could be the more subtle, "I'm with you, but only until another offer comes from elsewhere." For me, it often plays out like this:

Actual conversation

Friend: Anyway, then my boss says to me …

[Beep Beep]

… sorry, do you mind if I take this?

Me: Why, no. Of course not. Go ahead.

Conversation in my head

Me: Actually, yes, I do mind. After all, whoever it is hasn't made the effort to be with you in person. But I have. What more do I need to do to get your full attention? Should I go away from here and phone you? Would *that* help?!

Thank goodness I'm too polite to do this. I just need counselling for the bitterness.

Anyway, the point is: technology has made it easier to be distracted from the people around us. The way many of us work now – constantly monitoring our phones/emails/etc. – has made this a way of life. Linda Stone, a former vice president at Microsoft, has called it "continuous partial attention." It's "the behavior of continuously monitoring as many inputs as possible, paying partial attention to each."[2]

> Continuous partial attention is an always on, anywhere, anytime, any place behavior. It's neuro-chemically addictive, and it involves an artificial sense of constant crisis. We keep a top priority in focus. At the same time, we scan the periphery to see if we are missing other opportunities, and if we are, our very fickle attention shifts focus. What's ringing? Who is it? What email just came in? 15 text messages. Blog this. What time is it in Beijing, 19 voice mails....
>
> Overwhelm, overstimulation, and lack of fulfillment are the shadow side of our desire to connect and our always-on Age of Attention.[3]

Of course, it's not all about technology. The French film *Amélie* delightfully illustrates the other kinds of distraction. Almost its entire gallery of characters find ways to miss the beauty of each passing moment.

Raphael Poulain (Amélie's father) is lost in anxiety.

Madeleine (her neighbour) is trapped in the past.

Georgette (her colleague) is obsessed with her health.

Joseph (at her café) has become embittered by jealousy.

Monsieur Collignon (her grocer) is consumed by spiteful prejudice.

The ticket inspector on the Metro has no time for poetry.

A dancer at the sex shop is told about a mystery woman and gives a telling reply: "You won't find any mystery here."

Only Lucien, the local grocer's simple assistant, seems able to grasp the wonder of daily life. In one scene he delivers some groceries to a housebound man, Raymond Dufayel. Raymond complains that the groceries are so ordinary, but then Lucien makes his move. He lifts up the milk carton to reveal that it is only a facade. Underneath is a bottle of champagne. In fact, hidden beneath all the "boring" groceries lies a lovingly disguised collection of delicacies waiting to be unveiled.

Isn't this how it is in life? The spectacular is often hidden in the ordinary – if only we have eyes to see it.

Now, answering a mobile phone call or planning your evening while pretending to listen to your mother may not feel as careless as using a BlackBerry during sex. And probably it isn't. But it works in the same way. In each case we are passing up a wonderful gift for the sake of something much cheaper. Each person you meet today is a gift to you – sometimes their gift is a smile; sometimes it is to let you carry their shopping; sometimes it is to teach you patience – but they are always a gift.

If we are distracted, these gifts will pass us by.

▌Insulated from absence

When I was fifteen I went on a school adventure week to the Lake District in Northern England. The idea was to broaden our horizons and build character. One day the gruff games teacher, Mr Dorey, took a bunch of us for a walk round the lake known as Coniston Water. At a certain point, by the shore, he stopped us and got everyone to quieten down. The water lay mirror-still; beyond the tree-lined shore the hills rose gently up to a placid afternoon sky. "Listen," he said. "What can you hear?"

Silence.

"Exactly," he said.

It wasn't something we were used to. He might as well have shown us a three-headed goat or a piece of kryptonite. The truth is, like many teenagers, our lives were a journey from noise to noise. Being quiet or alone came close to the top of our list of Most Boring Things Ever. We were basically calmophobic.

Modern life is pretty well insulated from absence. We seldom have to be genuinely alone. The silence can be filled; the space can be crammed with activity. We have the Internet for company at home, music for the journey to work, the phone for the train.

We're so used to being contactable that some of us don't really like switching things off at all. How many of us leave a mobile phone on at night, even when we're sleeping? A youth worker I know confessed to not even switching his mobile phone off to pray. Is that really a good move if you believe in God? I mean, exactly what kind of person would you interrupt a conversation with God for? "Sorry, Almighty Creator, can I put you on hold? It's just that I think Cheryl wants to see if I've forgotten my gloves."

But constant noise and 24/7 availability is not the only way to live.

Q: What's the most important thing in music?

A: Silence.

Silence is the space that makes the notes special. Silence is the canvas on which the sound is painted.

A session musician once told me that the difference between an amateur and a pro is that a pro knows when *not* to play. And then what they do play is all the more significant.

Life is like this.

The silences are vital.

Thespacesmakelifemoreintelligible.

Many of us dread being bored, and we're offered a million ways to avoid it. But actually, boredom can be formative. It helps us to appreciate stimulation when it eventually comes. It opens our eyes to the realities around us. Not for nothing do bored kids on a car journey start to look out of the window and play I Spy.

If we can't deal with boredom, how will we accomplish anything that requires great concentration?

If we can't live with quietness, how can we hold our tongues when others need us to listen?

If we can't handle absence, what is our presence worth?

The mystery of you

Presence is irreplaceable. There's an intangible difference that our physical presence makes so that without it, nothing is quite the same. This is why emails cause so much misunderstanding. This is why so few people get married via videophone (you'd have to worry if your fiancée requested it).

I guess we could call it *the mystery of you*. There's something about you – you can't be captured in a thumbnail digital photo; you can't be summed up by a written résumé; you can't be fully heard over a phone line. You can only be truly enjoyed in the flesh.

It's as if we've been wired as a unity of soul and body, and anything less than our fully attentive bodily presence is just two-dimensional. It's like we've been made for presence.

When the early Christians claimed that God had come to this world, a vital part of their message was that he came in the flesh. They wrote:

> We proclaim to you the one who existed from the beginning, whom we have heard and seen. We saw him with our own eyes and touched him with our own hands.[4]

Somehow for God to send us a text message wouldn't have been enough. He certainly didn't just give out leaflets. He had to come and be present in the flesh. It only worked if God came in person, cleansing lepers with his own hands, reaching out to touch his followers when they were scared, sharing the warmth of a meal, breaking bread, washing feet.

This wasn't a risk-free strategy. Being in the flesh meant people could walk away from him. Or betray him with a kiss. Or nail him to a cross. Somehow only this would do.

Jesus knew all about the rhythms of presence and absence. He faithfully stuck with his little band of followers. Rulers desired an audience with him; crowds scoured the countryside for him. But often he wasn't interested. It was quality and depth he was after – sharing travels and tables and trials.

He knew how to be absent too. On more than one occasion, he was simply lost to the world. He would disappear to "lonely places" for time alone with his Father.[5] His life was punctuated by these times; like a pulse, like blood returning to and flowing from a heart. His absence empowered his presence.

There's a greatness in this freedom to be with others and yet also to leave them. It's something we could all do with. Dietrich Bonhoeffer, a German pastor involved in the resistance to Hitler, set up a community on these principles:

> Let him who cannot be alone beware of community. He will only do harm to himself and to the community.... You cannot escape from yourself; for God has singled you out....

> But the reverse is also true: Let him who is not in community beware of being alone.[6]

Here's the goal: to be able to be with others, fully and freely – and to be able not to. Anything less implies that our company is merely an escape from loneliness, or our solitude is just hiding from others. We were made for this greater life. No more dreaming of being somewhere else. No more twitching to check email. No more constantly craving background music.

So how do we do it?

||||||||||||||||||||||||||||||||||||||||||||||||||||||||||||||||||||||||||||||||||||||||

Being wanted

Do you have a mobile phone? If so, how do you feel when it rings?

OK, maybe sometimes we're irritated by our phones, but mostly we like it. There's a sugar buzz when our self-chosen ringtone sounds (a genius idea by phone designers). There's a frisson of excitement when the phone vibrates. This can be confusing. If I'm wearing my corduroy trousers, whenever they rub together it feels like someone's trying to reach me! And the most exciting thing of all: we are in demand. Someone wants to talk with you, to connect to you. You are *wanted*.

Being wanted is part of the telephonic ladder of desire.

The telephonic ladder of desire

The toddler's rattle – the phone is bright and colourful.

The child's toy – the phone lights up when it is touched; I am not allowed to use it; it gets my parents' attention.

The young adolescent's friend – the phone keeps me safe; I can speak to friends or family; it stops me from being bored.

The older adolescent's necessity – it connects me with my peers; it helps me share some of my life's significant moments; if I don't have a phone, I will be excluded.

The adult's compulsion – the phone links me with clients; it keeps my children safe; I manage my life through my phone; it saves me from loneliness.

Everyone wants to be wanted. Children crave attention. Kids want to be popular. Teenagers need to be included. Adults long to be kept in touch. At every level, mobile phones promise to answer this need. An Orange phone promotion campaign ran like this: "I am who I am because of everyone." Which prompts the question: If I'm not connected to others, am I anybody at all?

If that's true, we should stay in touch with the phone network at all costs.

But what if there's more to us than that?

In particular, what if there is a wanting that puts all other wantings in the shade?

What if we are wanted by Someone? Someone whose desire for us is steady and unyielding, more stable than any human wanting, despite knowing our worst failings. Yet this wanting doesn't seek to possess or control us; it seeks only our freedom and our flourishing.

This is how we are wanted by God.

Archbishop Rowan Williams describes what it's like to come into this truth:

> … you have to be utterly convinced that you exist because God wanted you to; and that because God wanted you to exist, he liked the thought of you. In which case, there's not much alternative, really, but to go along with what God wanted - i.e. to give thanks for being yourself and rejoice in it. Not in a way that says, I'm entirely fine, mature, virtuous, balanced, brave and modest - God doesn't like the thought of us because he admires us; he just likes the thought of this particular person, warts and all, existing as a place where glory may be visible. So when we delight in being ourselves, we're not passing an approving judgment on all we do and suggesting that we need no improvement and face no radical challenge, we're acknowledging with joy the fact of our unique existence, as willed by God.[7]

We are wanted by God – deeply, passionately, freely and joyfully. If this is how we are wanted, then we needn't crave social connection in the same way.

If this is true, then there is a message we need to receive each day *before* we receive all the others. This is how Jesus began things. Not just in the quietness at the dawn of the day, but also at the very start of his public work, he began with the words spoken over him by God: "You are my Son, the Beloved, with you I am well pleased."[8]

Jesus began with the Yes of God. Everything else he did or said flowed from being rooted in the loving desire of the God he knew as Father.

Each day we live can begin in the same way. It's amazing to think that some of us who call ourselves Christians pay homage to the gods of *Ee'mayl* or *Mowb Eye-ul* before we listen for the voice of the Living God. But God issues a different invitation to us: to be present to him before being present to anyone else, so that his securing love can meet us ahead of whatever we will face that day.

The church I currently work for has a cavernous neo-Gothic structure for a building. A few years ago, we commissioned a huge altar background depicting the Father's welcome of a son who returns home, from the parable Jesus told. For months now, the very front of the church has been curtained off while the artist, Charlie Mackesy, completes his work.

Every Thursday morning, before my working day begins, I have the most incredible privilege. I sneak in behind the curtain, to the dim, secluded area where the painting is still in progress. And there, in the early calm, cut off from the world, I pray.

Standing in front of that vast canvas, prayer takes on new dimension. I am drawn into the embrace taking shape above me. I am the prodigal son, and God's forgiving arms are wrapped around me.

I know well that this embrace isn't cheap. The father in the story couldn't

This is the story of the prodigal son. It should really be called the running father – who waited every day for his boy to return. The boy who had rejected him so badly and finally, when he saw him from a long way off – his father ran to him and hugged him, and kissed him. Luke 15*

The Prodigal Son by Charlie Mackesy

have run out to hug his rebellious son without suffering the sting of shame.[9] No matter. Love is willing to pay the price.

And so I stand there and let myself be loved at great cost. I wait there quietly and let myself be found. I pour out my heart until there are no words left, safe in the knowledge that I am wanted.

Then, and only then, I turn on my phone.

▌Allowing absence

My phone has a button on it that accesses the Internet. The button is called Planet 3. Like it's not a button; it's a *world*. They're nearly right, though. There is a button on the phone that opens up a new world:

Off.

I'm not saying that technology is a bad thing. Not at all. But technology is at its best when it serves the rhythms of life. Breathing apparatus for premature babies. An answerphone safeguarding meal times. This is where technology supports the rhythm, gracefully tucking itself into the background of our lives, which are richer as a result.

Technology makes us poorer when it interrupts life. For that reason, sometimes (regularly, in fact) technology serves us best by going on vacation.

We all need time to be absent. Orange is wrong (again): you can be who you are when no one is there. Who you are is a generous gift that doesn't depend on the size of your inbox.

Sometimes we need to be bored or lonely or lost, and there's no point just using people or things to cover it up. Those feelings can be important indicators of the true state of our lives. They can be homing signals that point us to God. They can be the crucible of the soul.

Absence has a unique spiritual purpose. You could say that God is like a hairdresser – he does some of his best work on us when we are still. Or you could say something more profound, like Mother Teresa:

> We need to find God, and he cannot be found in noise and restlessness. God is the friend of silence. See how nature – trees, flowers, grass – grow in silence; see the stars, the moon and sun, how they move in silence. We need silence to be able to touch souls.[10]

There's a profound picture of this in William P. Young's *The Shack*. In this novel, Mack, a man whose life has been shattered by grief, finds himself invited into an extended time of absence at a lakeside cabin. But the absence, for all its difficulty, is transformed by a meeting with Jesus. As the stillness does its work, the results are surprising:

> Night was falling quickly and the distant darkness was already thick with the sounds of crickets and bullfrogs. Jesus took his arm and led him up the path while his eyes adjusted, but already Mack was looking up into a moonless night at the wonder of the emerging stars.
>
> They made their way three-quarters up the dock and lay down on their

backs looking up. The elevation of this place seemed to magnify the heavens, and Mack reveled in seeing stars in such numbers and clarity.... It almost felt like he was falling up into space, the stars racing toward him as if to embrace him....

"Wow!" he whispered.

"Incredible!" whispered Jesus, his head near Mack's in the darkness....

In the silence that followed, Mack simply lay still, allowing the immensity of space and scattered light to dwarf him, letting his perceptions be captured by starlight and the thought that everything was about him ... about the human race ... that this was all for us. After what seemed like a long time, it was Jesus who broke into the quiet.

"I'll never get tired of looking at this. The wonder of it all – the wastefulness of creation, as one of our brothers has called it. So elegant, so full of longing and beauty even now."

"You know," Mack responded, suddenly struck anew by the absurdity of his situation; where he was; the person next to him. "Sometimes you sound so, I mean, here I am lying next to God Almighty and, you really sound, so ..."

"Human?" Jesus offered. "But ugly." And with that he began to chuckle, quietly and restrained at first, but after a couple of snorts, laughter simply started tumbling out. It was infectious, and Mack found himself swept along, from somewhere deep inside. He had not laughed from down there in a long time.... Mack felt more clean and alive and well than he had since ... well, he couldn't remember since when.

Eventually, they both calmed down again and the night's quiet asserted itself once more. It seemed that even the frogs had called it quits. Mack lay there realizing he was now feeling guilty about enjoying himself, about laughing, and even in the darkness he could feel *The Great Sadness* roll in and over him.

"Jesus?" he whispered as his voice choked. "I feel so lost."

A hand reached out and squeezed his, and didn't let go. "I know, Mack. But it's not true. I am with you and I'm not lost."[11]

Absence may be quiet, but it isn't tame. It's the doorway to the inside of our lives. It is wild and beautiful and sometimes humourous. And it can be the place for real, honest meeting with God.

▌Pursuing presence

This is the journey I want to go on: to be simply who I am, in presence and in absence, in one place at a time. As the missionary Jim Elliot put it, "Wherever you are, be all there."

So what am I learning about being present?

I am learning to give time. We are much better today at connecting to others than committing to them. We rack up "friends" on social networking sites. We spread our presence thinly among hundreds of contacts. We maintain relationships round the country and the globe, but we don't always get to know people where we live. Commitment, time, being *on time* – these are the raw materials out of which the magic of presence is woven.

I am learning to give attention. My full attention (remember what that was?). In our distracted age, Linda Stone calls this "the real aphrodisiac." This is a costly, delicate business, as William Barclay once explained:

> There are different kinds of listening. There is the listening of criticism; there is the listening of resentment. There is the listening of superiority; there is the listening of indifference. There is the listening of the man who only listens because for the moment he cannot get the chance to speak. The only listening that is worthwhile is the listening which listens and learns.[12]

I am learning to give freedom. Not to have an agenda for others. Not to consume them like a character in my own soap opera. To see the mystery of who they are – unrepeatable and uncontrollable. This includes coming to appreciate all their high-resolution weaknesses, their full-colour uniqueness and 3-D differences of opinion. Real relationship is not fantasy. It is slow and at times unsatisfying. But it is real, and that makes all the difference.

And I am learning to give myself. To be vulnerable and open. To be willing to be changed by the people I meet. The best encounters in the human drama are unscripted on both sides.

This is a much sharper reality than any sofa-bound home entertainment. Or, as wildlife journalist Simon Barnes put it: Life – it's the thinking person's television.

There is a high-definition world waiting each day for us to explore.

All we need to do is use the Power button.

Just not in the way we've been told.

CHAPTER 8

▌The Art of Waiting
(Wait & Enjoy)

You will think I'm mad.

I was having my breakfast while reading the Bible one day, and I looked out of the back window to see leaves falling from a tree in our yard.

I felt a strange compulsion to go outside and catch a falling leaf.

But unlike my normal leaf-catching urge (which is pretty much an annual affair), this seemed to come from – well, from God. Don't be silly, I thought. Get back to your Bible reading. But the Bible reading didn't help. It just said, "See to it that you do not refuse him who speaks." Spooky. So I did.

Like I said – mad.

So there I stood, on my back patio, waiting under a tree to catch a leaf for the Lord. And do you know what happened next?

The wind dropped.

Suddenly there was no leaf action at all. What will the neighbours think? How long could I be out here for? What a waste of time. My cornflakes will go soggy.

And so it went.

One or two leaves rushed down at something approaching the speed of sound. I wasn't going to get out of it that easily.

I waited some more …

Please, God, make this quick.

Then I felt the same divinely guided impulse again: Do you see how hard it is for you to wait? What have you got to do today that is more important than following me?

Nothing, I suppose. So I stood there some more and wished with all my heart that God could make me a patient man. Help me. Save me from self-importance and rush.

A calmness came to me from nowhere (or from Somewhere, depending on your point of view).

And soon the leaves started to fall again.

I caught one (good job – otherwise I could still be there now). And I went inside to chew on the problem of patience and some very soggy cereal.

||||||||||||||||||||||||||||||||||||||||||||||||||||||||||||||||||||||||||||||||||||||

▌On demand

How did we get so impatient?

Maybe we learn it by watching our parents drive.

Or maybe it's just part of living in an on-demand culture, where the pace of life has got faster and faster, and we expect everything to happen at our convenience. Call it Hurry Sickness; call it Time Poverty – whatever it is, we've got it.

There was a time when the fastest we could travel was riding a horse (except maybe by falling, but does that count as travel?). Now even the speed limits on our roads are too slow for us.

According to the latest statistics (who measures these things?), we now walk 10 percent faster than we did a decade ago. Not only does this give us less time to think; we look sillier too!

In many places around the world, eating meat is a privilege to look forward to. But in Western countries we do it without thinking. Our hamburgers arrive over the counter before there's even time to say grace.

For years, the radio has let us enjoy recorded music. But now, unless we own the tracks so that we can hear the right song in the right place at the right time, we're not satisfied.

We expect things instantly: quick, click. It's ours. Everything is faster, but we feel more pressured and stressed. We have more food than ever, but it is making us overweight and unwell.

There's something darker going on here too. In an on-demand world, we don't know how to deal with lack. Suffering, deprivation or loss is our collective nightmare. We play out our nightmare scenarios in fascinating but frightening news headlines or the "pain porn" of horror movies. But all the time we hope to God it never happens to us. We'll do anything to minimize pain, to reduce risk, and to protect ourselves from the sufferings of others.

Christians can be like this as well. Eugene Peterson notices in some churches "the refusal to be silent, the obsessive avoidance of emptiness, the denial of any experience and any people in the least suggestive of god-forsakenness."[1]

Can we be blamed for this? Perhaps not. We're trying to make our lives safe and satisfying, and we think the key is to maximize pleasure and minimize pain – to get what we want as soon as possible and cut out the dead time. On the face of it, this makes sense.

Anyway, what's the alternative?

Still life

Patience. It's the name of a card game you play on your own – that doesn't help its image. But patience is vital for appreciating life.

An on-demand lifestyle is not the right way to appreciate anything. I've heard there are tourists who go Paris, queue up outside the Louvre, and once inside head straight for the *Mona Lisa*. When they get there, they video the painting for about five seconds, then walk straight out of the building.[2] *Mona Lisa* done. Where next?

Some of us approach life like this. We look for the quick payoff, the easy win, and we rush straight from A to Z in pursuit of our final destination.

But art is not like that.

Art is about waiting (literally, standing still and watching). And waiting is an art. We have to pay attention, to give time for beauty's wings to unfurl. If we rush, we will miss what's there.

Q: What's the difference between a bus stop and an art gallery?

A: Nothing much. It's just that we pay better attention in an art gallery.

▌The impossible feast

Waiting is the key to all lasting enjoyment. Imagine, for instance, that every single day we could have our fill of the finest food imaginable, overload on dessert and wash it all down with plenty of wine/beer/cola (delete as applicable). Would that make every day a feast?

No. I imagine that most of us would enjoy Day One to Day Seven. Anytime between Week Two and Week Four, each meal would start to fade into all the others. After a while, we'd barely be able to appreciate any of the luxuries we had. By Month Six, we'd probably be bored, sick or deceased!

OK, it's an extreme example, but is it really so far from what our daily lives are like? Compared to most people in the world and in history, we feast every day. But it doesn't feel like it.

Here's the principle: For any day to really be a feast, some days can't be a feast. There's a rhythm of life here – waiting and enjoying. When M. Scott Peck wrote famously about taking "the road less traveled," he argued that to grow in freedom and maturity we need to learn to wait, to defer pleasure:

> Delaying gratification is a process of scheduling the pain and pleasure of life in such a way as to enhance the pleasure by meeting and experiencing the pain first and getting it over with. It is the only decent way to live.[3]

Waiting and enjoying belong together as part of the same picture. If we never experience any delay or lack, our lives are poorer for it. Wendy Mogel, a child psychologist in Los Angeles, saw how this worked with children from some of the most affluent families in the U.S. Why, she asked, were these kids so unhappy? She concludes in her book *The Blessing of a Skinned Knee*:

Unsure how to find grace and security in the complex world we've inherited, we try to fill up the spaces in our children's lives with stuff: birthday entertainments, lessons, rooms full of toys and equipment, tutors and therapists. But material pleasures can't buy peace of mind, and all the excess leads to more anxiety – parents fear that their children will not be able to sustain this rarified lifestyle and will fall off the mountain the parents have built for them.

In their eagerness to do right by their children, parents not only overindulge them materially but they spoil them emotionally. . . .

Deprived of opportunities to wait and dream and long for something, they never learn to value their possessions or experiences. Everything carries the same weight, and none of it weighs very much.[4]

It's a paradox. If every meal is a feast, no meal is a feast. If we want for nothing, we end up missing what we need most.

The ability to wait is a mark of maturity. Waiting builds our soul capacity. It enables us to carry tension. The problems of life and the ups and downs of human relationships will demand this of us.

If we can't wait, how can we have the perseverance to confront life's challenges?

If we can't wait, how can we avoid overwhelming the ones we love with our demands?

That's why the God of the Bible is a waiting God. He knows the pain of patience. He carries the tension of hope for a broken world. He's a spurned lover, a tireless dreamer and a lovelorn parent. It's a costly path, but this is the price of relationship. History shows that he chose this rather than overwhelm us with his purity and justice. One of Peter's New Testament letters reads: "He's restraining himself on account of you, holding back the End because he doesn't want anyone lost. He's giving everyone the time and space to change."[5] Because he loves, he waits.

▌ Practicing patience

How do we grow in patience?

Well, there's nothing for growing in patience like ...

Wait for it ...

Patience. As Rick Warren writes, "God develops the fruit of the Spirit in your life by allowing you to experience circumstances in which you're tempted to express *the exact opposite quality*! ... Patience is developed in circumstances in which we're forced to wait and are tempted to be angry or have a short fuse."[6]

Occasionally human beings buy into the myth that we control time. We talk about "time management" as if we can create, or move around, even a millisecond of time. The reality is that time is something that happens to us. We can't manipulate it; we can only learn to live in it. That means learning to wait.

If only there was a daily school of waiting. If only we had regular opportunities to practice patience.

Ah, but we do! Queues.

Despite the speed of modern life, we still find ourselves waiting in line, stuck in traffic or (everybody's favourite) on hold at the end of a phone. The pace of modern life makes even these short stops painfully slow. But what if we saw queues not as an inconvenience but as a gift? What if we took them as moments to pause and be thankful?

If you want to be forced to learn patience, go to Italy. Italian "queuing" (I use the word loosely) is a kind of free-form contact sport. Provided you make it out of an Italian queue alive, you'll certainly have learnt more about patience. Wherever we practice patience, though, the main thing is this: whatever makes us wait can also make us grow.

So how can we build a rhythm of waiting and enjoying into our lives?

IIIIIIIIIIIIIIIIIIIIIIIIIIIIIIIIIIIIIIIIIIIIIIIIIIIIIIIIIIIIIIIIIIIIIIIIIIIIIIIIIII

▌Pause before you buy

For most well-trained consumers, buying is a reflex reaction. Like laboratory dogs conditioned to salivate at the sound of a bell, as soon as we know what we want, we buy. The product can be ours in a matter of seconds. Marketeers know the importance of closing a deal as soon as possible (Click here to go to checkout/Buy now; pay later/What can I do to convince you to make the purchase today, madam?).

But waiting cuts the nerve of impulse purchasing. It buys us time. It allows us to change the consumer script and improvise something new.

The great spiritual writer Richard Foster makes the suggestion like this:

> I propose an exercise which many have found liberating. When you decide that it is right for you to buy a particular item, see if God will not bring it to you without your having to buy it....
>
> Once a decision is made to secure a particular item, hold it before God in prayer for perhaps a week. If it comes, bless God; if not, reevaluate your need for it; and if you still feel you should have it, go ahead and purchase the item.
>
> One clear advantage to this approach is that it effectively ends all impulse buying. It gives time for reflection so that God can teach us if the desire is unnecessary. Another obvious benefit is the way in which it integrates the life of devotion with the life of service. The supply of our material needs becomes an exciting venture of faith.[7]

So we decided to try this. For each purchase (except food, emergency medical supplies, etc.) we decided to wait a fortnight. The two weeks would allow us to think: Do we need this? Is it a good purchase for others and for the environment? Could we borrow it or make do without? And we would pray that somehow we wouldn't have to buy it.

Was it an "exciting venture of faith"? Actually, yes.

Our first test came with the slow demise of our television. It had been on the blink for a while. We had to teach our kids to strike it in just the right place whenever the screen inexplicably went blank. After a few weeks, a friend was round at our house and noticed the children repeatedly assaulting the TV set. Moved with compassion for our television, she offered us her own TV that she wasn't using anymore.

When our video recorder died we prayed again, and within the fortnight–without any prompting–my neighbour offered us a video and a telly. I said to her, "You'll never guess what: I've actually been asking God for this!" (She's not a Christian, but she probably wasn't fazed by this. If you've seen your neighbour waiting to catch a leaf in his backyard, why be surprised at anything?)

Not everything was given to us. When our vacuum cleaner broke (what's wrong with our house?), a family member offered to buy us a new one. We ended up waiting five years to buy a digital camera, but as a result we spent half as much. Sometimes we buy; sometimes we don't. But now, when we buy, it's with a much greater appreciation of the privilege of being able to purchase.

How to enjoy one person

Consuming is not the same as enjoying.

Example: Have you ever wolfed down a bar of chocolate?

It is possible to consume whole packs of confectionary without appreciating, or even really enjoying, the contents (believe me, I've done it). Most chocolate affairs are a brief encounter. Every bar is pretty much the same as all the rest. Consume, discard packaging.

That's OK as far as it goes, but it isn't true enjoyment. If something is worth enjoying, it's worth enjoying well.

True enjoyment takes time. When you really enjoy something, you start to uncover what in particular makes it special. Think of a child's favourite holiday location, a beloved family pet or the lifelong study of a style of music. This kind of enjoyment gets richer with time. The more we know, the more we value. The idea of swapping for something else doesn't come into it. Love makes what we love unique.

Now, nothing is worth enjoying like another person. And there's nothing so delightfully unique as the human body.

So what is the best way to enjoy another person?

Is it to pick them up for one night, like sweets from a vending machine? Consume, discard. Is it to switch to a new partner when a better-packaged offer comes along? Or is there a better way?

You might be thinking: Why are we talking about sex here? What on earth has sex got to do with consumerism?

Exactly. Too much.

Sex has become consumerized. It has become a product to use in pursuit of a maximized life. Reduced to technique, like a golf class. Reduced to orgasm, like a miracle bathroom cleaner that "does the job." Protected by consumer rights – wherever, whatever, whoever. Instead of waiting to enjoy one person, and only one person, in ever-increasing tenderness and depth, we're encouraged to consume a range of partners whenever the opportunity is there.

But without the rhythm of waiting and enjoying, sexual encounters blur into each other and never truly satisfy. Consumer sex can't do justice to the goods.

The alternative is covenant love. Covenant love is fierce, exclusive and lifelong:

> For love is as strong as death,
> its jealousy unyielding as the grave.
> It burns like blazing fire,
> like a mighty flame.
> Many waters cannot quench love;
> rivers cannot wash it away.
> If one were to give
> all the wealth of his house for love,
> it would be utterly scorned.[8]

This is what it takes to enjoy the inexhaustible wonder of one person. Covenant love is emigration to their territory, not tourism. And once we're there, it calls for faithful, delicate, passionate exploration. Married couples take note: when it comes to sex, sloppy disregard or thoughtless routine is not an option.

Consumerism can't cope with the no-returns policy of loving marriage. It baulks at the idea that any human being is worth limiting our options for. The risk is too great – consumerism folds. It doesn't know how to wait, and therefore it doesn't know how to enjoy.

Consumerism is OK for chocolate but not for love.

Fasting

If you want to catch the rhythm of waiting and enjoying, there's nothing like a fast.

Sometimes fasting can backfire. A friend of mine, for a host of devout reasons, decided that every Wednesday for a month he would consume nothing but water. So far, so good. However, later that month, his job took him to Brussels to organize a conference at one of the best hotels in Europe.

"Seeing as you are considering a major booking with us," said the maître d', "please feel free to order anything you wish from our menu, entirely on the house."

It was a Wednesday. Tough one.

"I'd just like some water, please."

"Is sir sure? Really, you can order anything you desire. Anything!"

"Yes, I'm sure. Water would be … just … fine."

Normally fasting isn't quite that painful. In fact, it has a unique ability to help us appreciate what we have. It breaks the monotony of abundance and reminds us how blessed we are. For sheer enjoyment, there's nothing quite like the first meal after a fast.

Fasting is a strange gift: the gift of lack. In a funny way, consumerism offers us a dull, mid-range experience of life. We rarely do without, so we never hit rock bottom; but because our lives are so generally abundant, we never truly feast either. We stick to the average: shrink-wrapping our joy and medicating our sorrow.

But fasting brings us into an extreme and vibrant world. For a brief moment we are connected to those who have nothing. When we practice any kind of fast, we share in the world's waiting for wholeness and in God's longing to bring it. We groan, and God groans with us. We mourn, somehow believing that those who mourn will be blessed.[9]

This theme of vulnerability is crucial because simplicity is often sold as a journey to tranquil self-fulfilment. To judge by some self-help books, the aim is for our lives to become the spiritual equivalent of a posh furniture catalogue: sparse, stylish, uncluttered. But this kind of detachment is nothing but exotic escapism.

Jesus offers something else – an authentic life which is sometimes messy and complicated. It is painful, because the real world is painful. John Smith, an Australian biker and advocate for social justice, writes:

> It's definitely worth thinking more about pain to discover what a gift in fact it is to the human race.... I would even dare to claim that it is the greatest single gift we can have. It offers over-fed, over-counselled, and over-amused Westerners an opportunity to step outside their own psychological alienation and taste the suffering in the two-thirds world. It teaches us compassion – a word that literally means suffering with others. It teaches us vulnerability, too, without which there is no room for God to work in our lives ... "shattered glass reflects the most light."[10]

This sounds risky. How do we know that the pain won't overwhelm us?

Because Jesus invites us into a world of hope. A world where joy can follow agony as surely as Sunday follows Friday. And if pain can be transfigured like this, then we don't need to fear it. We can go without. We can wait, and God will be with us as we do.

And it doesn't end there. Every fast should end with a feast, which points forward to "the feast in the kingdom of God."[11] The last word is never fasting, but feasting. The last word is always hope.

❙ ENJOY – how to savour

I am a fan of spontaneous gift giving. Obviously it does depend slightly on what you give, as I realized one day with a friend of mine, Dave.

Dave: Hey, Mark, I was reading a book by Dostoyevsky the other day, and I thought of you.

Me: Really?

Dave: Yes. So I decided to buy you a copy as a gift.

Me: That's so nice of you! No one has ever bought me a book just because it made them think of me. What's it called?

Dave: *The Idiot.*

The idiot. I swallowed my pride and read the novel. And what a gift it was. The central character, Prince Myshkin (though how exactly he is a prince is never quite clear), is an idiot. That is, people think he is an idiot. But actually, he only looks strange to them because he is so much more alive than they are. In a society of greed and pretence, his life is utterly authentic. Part of his secret is to be present, not only to people, but also to *the moment*. He's not trapped in the past or lost in the future but fully and wondrously concentrated on his surroundings.

Early in the novel, the prince enters into a polite discussion with three aristocratic daughters. Adelaida, who loves to paint, asks him to teach her "how to look at things." The prince tells her how precious life has become to him, describing some of his experiences in luminous detail.

Then he illustrates with a story. The previous year he had met a man who had been sentenced to death for a political crime. The man was taken to his place of execution and waited there, with a few others, for certain death. However, after about twenty minutes, he was given a reprieve. What fascinated Prince Myshkin was that in those moments before the reprieve, the man experienced the passage of time with an extraordinary sharpness. The prince continues the story like this:

> "The priest went to each of them with the cross. It seemed to him then that he had only five more minutes to live. He told me that those five minutes were like an eternity to him, riches beyond the dreams of avarice; he felt that during those five minutes he would live through so many lives that it was quite unnecessary for him to think of the last moment, so that he had plenty of time to make all sorts of arrangements: he calculated the exact time he needed to take leave of his comrades, and that he could do that in two minutes, then he would spend another two minutes in thinking of himself for the last time, and, finally, one minute for a last look round.
>
> "He was dying at twenty-seven, a strong and healthy man; taking leave of his comrades, he remembered asking one of them quite an irrelevant question and being very interested indeed in his answer. Then, after he

had bidden farewell to his comrades, came the two minutes he had set aside for thinking of himself; he knew beforehand what he would think about: he just wanted to imagine, as vividly and as quickly as possible, how it could be that now, at this moment, he was there and alive and in three minutes he would merely be *something*–someone or something–but what? And where? All that he thought he would be able to decide in those two minutes! There was a church not far off, its gilt roof shining in the bright sunshine. He remembered staring with awful intensity at that roof and the sunbeams flashing from it; he could not tear his eyes off those rays of light: those rays seemed to him to be his new nature, and he felt that in three minutes he would somehow merge with them … The uncertainty and the feeling of disgust with that new thing which was bound to come any minute were dreadful, but he said that the thing that was most unbearable to him at the time was the constant thought, 'What if I had not had to die! What if I could return to life–oh, what an eternity! And all that would be mine! I should turn every minute into an age, I should lose nothing, I should count every minute separately and waste none!' He said that this reflection finally filled him with such bitterness that he prayed to be shot as quickly as possible."[12]

There's nothing like the threat of imminent death to focus the mind! But the prince's point here, which he lives out all through the novel, is that we can all live more deliberately and be less wasteful of the moments we are given. We can "count every minute separately."

There's no point in waiting if we don't also enjoy. We need to learn to let moments wash over us. We can learn to notice. We can savour. Mike Yaconelli puts it like this: "Savoring is the lost art of cherishing, appreciating, relishing. When you and I stop and savor a particular of life, we soak it in, we listen with all our senses, we immerse ourselves in what we are savoring."[13]

Savouring opens our eyes to little things.

Perhaps the toughest year of my life was unexpectedly lifted in an instant when one day I noticed the first crocus of spring. My gloom thawed. Hope in a flower.

More recently, we spent a noisy morning at the swimming pool with our kids and a friend who was awaiting brain surgery. The swimming was a good distraction, but it was nothing compared to the free lunchtime entertainment. As we sat with our sandwiches, we saw an old guy (and I mean old) step up to the highest diving platform and stand, a little unsteadily, at the end of the board. We worried for his life. But we needn't have. With the whole pool watching, he proceeded to pull off the most audacious stunt dive. Then he came back (slowly) for another, and another, and another. Everyone hooted with joy. Our day was graced.

This is so often how it works. Joy waits each day to be noticed. What we glimpse in our most profound moments is, in fact, always there. If we only learn to look.

And behind every savoured gift lies God, the Source. Dostoyevsky found him in the dazzling light refracting off the roof of a church. But we might find him anywhere. At any given instant, God is never far away. Some call this the sacrament of the present moment.[14]

Prince Myshkin discovered all this.

He learned how to look at things.

He spurned the conventions of society and determined to "count every minute separately."

But then Prince Myshkin was an idiot.

Wasn't he?

CHAPTER 9

The Deep Yes
(Shallow No & Deep Yes)

Let me tell you about the best Christmas I ever had. The best Christmas wasn't the one with the most presents. It wasn't the warmest, or even the whitest.

It was the one without electricity.

It happened while my parents lived in a tiny village out in the Cheshire countryside in the North West of England. Each year our family used to gather in their grand old vicarage for Christmas. The normal yuletide ritual was to hole ourselves up in various rooms; there were two different TV options running at the same time, the kitchen for snacks, the hall for phone calls round the country, or we could be quietly tucked away in centrally heated rooms. Then we'd come together for meals and a few special moments.

But one year that didn't happen. The icy cold, nature's emissary, had taken out a power line somewhere. So we were forced into different patterns. The lights went out. The TV rooms fell silent. Out came candles and kindling for the open fire. For the first time in a long time, we had to pull together as a family. What had effectively been a hotel became a home once again.

We spent the days in awe of winter's fierce grandeur. We passed our evenings sitting together round the fireplace, sharing inconveniences and swapping stories. The atmosphere was unforgettable. The Christmas film schedule passed us by completely. No one noticed.

Friends commiserated with our loss. Radio bulletins spoke with concern and pathos. But we were experiencing something different entirely. Part of our family was coming alive, just as somewhere in time a Saviour was being born.

For a long time, I chewed over what happened in those precious few days. It was a present we hadn't asked for, a reminder of what we once knew as children. Like anything with a hint of the sacred about it, putting the meaning into words isn't easy.

But to save this chapter from being a set of blank pages, I'm going to call it *deep*.

||||||||||||||||||||||||||||||||||||||||||||||||||||||||||||||||||||||||||||||||

▌Life on a shallow planet

How much of our time do we spend living through screens?

Phone screens, computer screens, TV screens, digital advertising boards. There's something about this that isn't ideal. It's an unavoidable part of modern life, but it doesn't feel like the fullness of what we've been made for. We end up living life at a distance. Like a brain in a jar, we are stimulated by signals and send responses, but don't actually get our hands on the real world.

There's something about our consumerized, technological world – a shallowness, a disconnection from our surroundings. This is easier to illustrate than explain.

Our first son was once given a shape sorter. Do you remember these? Squares through the square hole, triangles through the circle hole. ("Why doesn't it fit?" thinks the baby. "I'd better bash it harder.") Only this was a mega shape sorter – ten times better than the old wooden ones that kids used to play with. It was made of lightweight fluorescent plastic, and every time a shape passed through the right hole, it triggered a button that made lights flash and a little tune play. How stimulating! Babies must love this stuff, right? And it was educational too.

But it wasn't. The lightweight shapes were garish and bright, but they had no substance or texture, so they were actually less satisfying to touch than the wooden blocks they replaced. It wasn't long before Jonah worked out that the shapes were triggering a button somewhere. One afternoon I found him sitting motionless in the middle of the carpet, his eyes glazed, his face expressionless. He had his finger on the hidden button, and he was pressing it again and again and again. The tweeting ditty was playing over and over, and it would have continued like that until the batteries ran out or the electronics (inevitably) broke.

The toy was a generous present, but some gifts take away more than they give. It was stimulating but not satisfying. "Improved" but worse. It meant to inspire a tiny, inquisitive mind, but it just closed down his options and left him pressing buttons.

I couldn't help but notice the difference a few years later. My dad and I took Jonah and his brother Zach out to the local park. We saw them engaging in a much deeper way. Jonah knew how to recognize autumn, with its ochre-brown palette and grieving trees. We made great piles of leaves and took turns running and launching right into the middle of them. The two boys tumbled and dived together. We all took our turn, revelling in the exquisite abundance as the leaves exploded around us, and sensing the fragile crackle as they pressed against our skin.

This wasn't life through a screen. We were bodily alive, relationally alive, leafily alive. How can I express this? Can you see that I'm struggling?

Shallow versus deep

Thank goodness for the philosopher Albert Borgmann. I stumbled across his work as a student, and it changed the way I look at the world.

Borgmann pointed out the difference between things and commodities. The leaves were a "thing"; the shape sorter was a "commodity." A "thing" has what Borgmann calls a commanding presence. It is deep, rich, sensuous, real. A "commodity" is much less substantial. It is shallow, push button, undemanding, throwaway. The problem comes when our world becomes so full of commodities that they squeeze out the things that make life meaningful. Instead of a deep world of satisfying engagement, we end up with a shallow world of disposable stuff.

For example, think of the difference between a real fire and a radiator. Radiators are modern, efficient and useful. But whoever described a romantic break like this:

> I couldn't believe our luck when we went away last week – the cottage we stayed in had a *real radiator*. It was probably the highlight of our stay. In the early evening, David would get the radiator just right. Then later on,

we'd sit there for ages, telling stories round the radiator or just watching it late into the night. It was so romantic. When the mood took us, we threw caution to the wind and made love in front of an open radiator!

Now, no one is suggesting that we go back to living in forests round log fires. Nostalgia shouldn't blind us to the genuine improvements that technology has brought to our health and living conditions. But at the same time, just because the move to central heating has been beneficial, that doesn't mean *nothing has been lost along the way*. Everything has pros and cons, but what with hard-sell advertising and newfound convenience, we don't always take stock of what we are missing. In the case of fires, we've lost the beauty of a real flame; we've lost a family ritual; we've lost the active habit of preparing the fuel; we've lost a central gathering place in the home. Life has become shallower, and we may not have even noticed.

How can we spot the difference between the deep and the shallow?

Deep life is playing football with all comers in a local park. Shallow life is getting hooked on video "sports" games that can only parody the real thing.

Deep life is hearing a real-live musician, or making music yourself. Shallow life is pressing Play. How much time do we spend pressing Play rather than actually playing?

Deep life is fixing a fence and feeling proud because you toiled hard and worked out, with a little help from your neighbour, how to do it. Shallow life is plastic technology you didn't make, don't understand and can't mend.

Deep life is walking in local hills. Shallow life is a mountain screen saver.

Deep life breaks out spontaneously when the snow falls, and we find ourselves watching out for each other in the street and launching impromptu snowball fights. Shallow life stays indoors.

Deep life isn't just about the thing itself; it's about the effect it has. Deep life brings the best out of us: it requires exertion and practice. It brings the best out of others: we spend time in their company or pick up from them traditions and expertise. It brings the best out of nature: we experience it firsthand in all its grit and glory.

The problem with shallow life is that it so quickly becomes full. All our commodities are expensive. We work hard to afford them and shop long to find them. Shallow stuff is easy and often mildly addictive. It's not that we don't want to go out and "get a life"; we just find that we don't have time – or we're exhausted, and it's just so much easier to slump into the sofa. Over time, if we're not careful, we lose more and more of the skills we need to approach life deeply. The park empties as too many people are stuck indoors. We grow unfit, and so football is no longer an option. We're too pressed for time to learn an instrument, so all we can do is use our sound systems. We no longer talk to our neighbours, so they can't help us fix the fence.[1]

Here's the rhythm at stake: shallow no; deep yes. The way into a richer existence is to find ways to reduce the shallowness of our lives and embrace the things that make them deeper.

But the good news is: a deeper life isn't hard to find, as journalist Sarfraz Manzoor discovered with home cooking:

> I used to consider food to be little more than fuel; takeaways and pasta were the dull but reassuringly time-efficient staples of my diet.... Having tired of the rubbish I was eating, I resolved to start learning some of my mother's recipes....
>
> The great appeal of cooking is that while you can have a virtual friend and play online scrabble, you cannot cook a virtual saag aloo. The sensation of chopping and slicing and stirring, the smell of chilli powder and tandoori masala as it simmers with the olive oil and chopped tomatoes and onions and potatoes are all so gloriously real – and they demand one is engaged in the living moment....
>
> [Cooking] is not only creative, it also encourages social interaction: when

I ate takeaways I ate alone, now that I cook I want to invite others to share my food. When so much of modern life is passive, cooking demands an active engagement with the present, and it reminds us that life is not a spectator sport—it is there to be savoured.[2]

Now you might be thinking, this sounds interesting, but what has it got to do with God?

Does God do home cooking? Does he care if we go to the park or not?

Where is God in all this?

Right in the middle of it. God made us for more than a shallow life. He's the creator of the physical world, and he wants us to find bodily satisfaction in it. He cares about relationship too (as a trinity of Father, Son, and Spirit, he *is* relationship). It's no surprise that this God calls together a community—his church. And what do they do? They meet in the flesh, make music, share food, engage with their neighbourhood and cherish their world. You can't do virtual church, not really.

God made us to grow. He made us to be stretched and matured as we find our place in the world. Technology can be part of this, part of our development, but it can also get in the way.

The danger of technology is that we try to control the world. We maximize consistency; we eliminate risk; we tailor everything to the lone individual. Thermostat, insurance, GPS. We no longer need others; we no longer depend on life's kindness. We are safe, cocooned, in control.

But life, and the God who gave it, calls us out from these defences. Into a world that requires physical effort but repays it with hard-won satisfaction. A world where we need others and are needed by them in return but through this learn the meaning of love. Where we face the fragility of our lives but glimpse the wild wonder of the planet we inhabit.

In this deep world God is easier to find. We find ourselves smaller and more vulnerable. But this is ideal. God has special concern for the small and the vulnerable.

||||||||||||||||||||||||||||||||||||||||||||||||||||||||||||||||||||||||||||||||||||

▌Deep yes 1: childhood

We learn the deep things of life in childhood. Children have a natural affinity for picking up new skills and making new connections. Most powerful of all, they possess imagination by the bucketload.

But one feature of consumerism is the way it crowds out children's innate desire to engage imaginatively with their world. Their parents are busy; the outside world is unsafe; they rarely face extended times of boredom. Filling children's worlds with digital entertainment may keep them occupied, but it also squeezes the space they need to be creative. Children's author Jacqueline Wilson put it like this:

> We are not valuing childhood. I speak to children at book signings and they ask me how I go through the process of writing and I say, "Oh you know, it's just like when you play imaginary games and you simply write it all down." All I get is blank faces. I don't think children use their imaginations any more.[3]

Imagination houses the riches of the human mind. It's like a computer processor – the larger it is, the more creative we can be. But the more children simply gaze at a screen, the less adept they become at creating their own images.

Why is imagination so much under threat?

The average child spends something like fifty hours a week in front of a screen, and that figure is rising. Fifty hours. That's a long time. I mean, *really* long. No, but really, it is. I could go on about this. I could go on about this for fifty hours (would that be a long time?). I wonder how it compares to the amount of time kids get with their parents. If it doesn't compare well, then who is really bringing up our kids? The majority of children have TVs in their rooms and watch TV with their evening meal and also before they go to bed.[4]

Now, some children's TV is better than it used to be. You can't see the strings on the puppets, for starters. But television watching has been linked with problems such as hyperactivity and obesity in some children.[5] The quick shot changes diminish concentration. The glossy images form a fake celebrity world. I suppose it's called "children's programming" for a reason – it shapes their minds.

In 2006, a group of British writers, teachers, sports coaches and psychologists decided that enough was enough. They wrote a letter to a national newspaper calling for a new approach to raising children:

> Since children's brains are still developing, they cannot adjust – as full-grown adults can – to the effects of ever more rapid technological and cultural change. They still need what developing human beings have always needed, including real food (as opposed to processed "junk"), real play (as opposed to sedentary, screen-based entertainment), firsthand experience of the world they live in, and regular interaction with the real-life significant adults in their lives.[6]

Real food, real play, real life and time with the adults they love. That's a deep childhood. Why wouldn't we want children to have this?

Let me say how this works for us (six years into the parenting roller coaster). We do have a TV, but only one, and there are limits about watching it (at the moment it's about five hours a week). We encourage the kids to make and draw and read and, yes, sometimes to be bored. We can't avoid the shallow stuff of life; in fact, sometimes it's lots of fun. But we try to invest in the deep world, to make it as big and real as possible. Whatever the age and stage kids are at, there must be ways to do this.

The other week, Jonah said to me, "Dad, I want a brand-new bike [he'd never used the term *brand-new* before – he's catching on!]. My bike is for babies, and Tom's has special shocks on the front." On the one hand, everything within me as a father wanted to go out that weekend and buy a brand-new shiny bike with huge shock absorbers whose enormity is eclipsed only by their pointlessness. And maybe one day I will. But I don't want to teach my son that satisfaction lies in just popping to the shops and buying brand-new things. So I asked myself, "How can I invest in the deep world?"

Here's what we did. We named his bike (Blue Thunder, and mine is Black Lightning – nobody mess with us!). I told him stories about the adventures our bikes could have, and he drew a picture. But most of all, I set aside an afternoon to go outside with him to clean it, oil it and show him how it works. All along, I knew that spending time on the bike *together* made it special. As best I could, I invested in the world of imagination, creativity and partnership. And it paid off. Later that week, during one of Blue Thunder's more dangerous missions, he cried out, "I love my bike!"

Deep yes 2: news

The news is vital, isn't it?

It's good to be kept in touch. It's important to know what's going on around us.

There's just one problem. The news is not the news.

What we call "news" is probably better called the *Daily Spectacle*. It's less about events, more about entertainment. It comes to us edited, packaged and ready to be consumed in the most exciting format. The *NBC Nightly News* theme, for instance, was written by film composer John Williams. It was described by comedian Bill Bailey in his show "Bill Bailey's Remarkable Guide to the Orchestra," as "pure Hollywood entertainment. It sounds like ET on a horse being chased by Darth Vader."[7]

The ingredients of modern TV "news" are known to us all:

How to make TV "news"

Be shocking—man eats own head.

Keep shifting the focus—this week Indonesia, next week Malawi, after that Russia, Brazil, New Zealand and China (in no particular order).

Keep it simple—man in suit says the new law is wrong, woman on street says it is right, cut to next item …

Image is everything—nothing is allowed to "happen" unless there can be a shot of a reporter standing somewhere on location to talk about it.

Pursue the public interest—it is essential to broadcast pictures of people's unusual medical conditions, the latest celebrity gossip or footage of bizarre pets. The public has a right to know.

Stay impartial—if the latest news happens to be a film premiere, product launch or sports event, so be it. For some inexplicable reason this isn't just free advertising.

Of course, nothing hits the headlines like a disaster. Disasters are image-led, exhilarating, fearsome and tragic. They can unfold over several days like a serial drama; they introduce us to new heroes and villains; they sell papers and keep us glued to our screens. But how many disasters are too many?

What is the point of us watching these scenarios in location after location with no real connection to people or places, except at the very most a brief charitable donation to an emergency appeal?

What could be the effect of constant immersion in this kind of "news"?

We become helpless viewers. We are drawn in by fascination but rarely engaged in any lasting way. Vincent Miller writes:

> Human suffering is neither ignored nor comprehended …; rather, it is packaged and sold as media spectacle.… A character in Don DeLillo's novel *Mao II* speaks of "the emergence of news as an apocalyptic event … our desperation has led us toward something larger and darker. So we turn to the news, which provides an unremitting mood of catastrophe. This is where we find emotional experience not available elsewhere."…

The news media are not in the business of analyzing causes and promoting debate on solutions. Rather, it is a marketer of intensities, of which the suffering other is a best-selling variety.... In the absence of analysis of [suffering's] causes and proposals to address it, it merely stupefies.[8]

TV news in particular makes us pessimistic and fearful. After watching thirty minutes of TV news footage, volunteers in an experiment described feeling "depressed, confused, irritated, angry, and anxious."[9] This, in turn, makes us more likely to spend time safely indoors.

The news is restless. Even if there's nothing actually worth reporting, it never stops. It was not always like this — once, on April 18, 1930, the BBC reported absolutely no news whatsoever and replaced its bulletin with some light piano music! Imagine that sense of calm descending on the news media now.

I should add here: it is certainly important to have informed concern for the wider world. Our prayers, our consumer choices and our votes have a huge influence on the globe. But there's more than one way to do this, and the daily news doesn't always help. As American writer Ben Hecht said, "Trying to determine what is going on in the world by reading newspapers is like trying to tell the time by watching the second hand of a clock."

So what is the alternative to the daily "news" the media feeds us?

There's a place for in-depth reading. There's a place for developing long-term relationships with communities around the world. There's a place for real political engagement that goes beyond slogans. But the true opposite of the daily spectacle is much closer to home: real community.

Think about the birth of a baby. It rarely hits the headlines (unless the birth takes place up a tree in the middle of a flood). But a new baby is among the best news some people ever have. And it's not just a private event either. Family and friends offer congratulations; strangers in the street offer compliments; neighbours offer help. For once we have a reason to need each other.

How ironic that the most newsworthy things in our lives never make the news. And there are more of these moments out there, waiting just outside our front doors for us to share, but we're too busy following "the news" to go out and find them!

So what is the news? Is it this week's massacre, tonight's scandal, next weekend's sporting event?

No. The news is where we live and who we know.

Even if I just take one street where we lived as an example. Up the road are Sam and Fortune, who met in Tanzania, where her grandmother still lives. They have a young family with three delightful girls (who have plenty of entertaining stories to share as they grow up). Another household is dealing with the painful aftermath of debt and separation. Round the corner lives a kindly old lady who has outlived her son and most days wanders aimlessly into town. Down the road in the local flats, a drug addict has come to faith. Her neighbour is an alcoholic who needs help decorating his house. And so on.

Just one small area. There is so much quietly unfolding joy, so much call for neighbourliness and practical help.

This is the news. This is the deep local world waiting for us. Here ends the bulletin.

Deep yes 3: relationships

Relationships struggle to grow in the thin soil of consumer life. Time is short and overloaded with options. We move around more and commit to others less. Today the average American has only two close friends, and almost one in four has no one to confide in at all.[10] The same thing is happening all over.

Our relationships get channelled into shallow patterns. We trade opinions via anonymous chat sites, under the cover of our "user name."

We get hooked on the artificial world of TV drama (yes, even the gritty, "realistic" kind). We become armchair experts on gangster culture, the inner workings of the White House, counterterrorism or whatever else is featured in the latest unmissable series. Season one, season two, season three—we get drawn into the long narrative arc. But in the process we lose time to enjoy the drama in our own lives and neighbourhoods.

Then there's porn.

The current Archbishop of Canterbury once wrote that porn "is not erotic enough." If this was a formal complaint to an adult film company, I'd be concerned, but it was actually in a work of theology.[11] And he's right.

Real sex—sex as the tender mystery God intended—is intimate, patient, focussed on the other. It's tricky (to friends about to get married I liken it to learning to play the guitar!). It can be frustrating. But it binds two souls together and whispers the irreducible worth of the one you love.

Porn is nothing like this. It's quick, cheap and easily forgotten. Porn is lonely—it takes place in pornonymity. It speaks of nobody's worth, which is why it makes us feel so guilty. Porn is not sexy enough by half.

Porn is shallow—it can't deliver the real human connection it promises. One adult show (in a rather transparent attempt to appear "cultural") did a feature on a pornographic sculptor. The interviewer wanted to know why he used such soft rock for his work. "Why aren't there many naked sculptures in granite?" she asked. The sculptor replied, "Sculpting in granite is expensive, difficult, and time-consuming."

Enough said.

Ironically this was probably one of the most revealing moments that show has ever broadcast.

Why do we get drawn into this stuff? Why does Saturday night find men glued to sporting highlights instead of embracing their wives? Why are some young couples so used to leisure time that having kids feels like a sacrifice? Why is it so hard to commit to one area and the people we meet there?

It doesn't have to be this way. We can grow deep relationships. We can invest in our family and, perhaps, embark on the risky journey of marriage and raising kids. We can build friendships; we can share meals; we can commit to a local church. All it takes is a shallow no and a deep yes.

||||||||||||||||||||||||||||||||||||||||||||||||||||||||||||||||||||||||||||

The burning yes

How do we cultivate a deep life?

We can't just bolt deep things onto our overcrowded schedules. There's a rhythm. We need to reduce or minimize a shallow aspect of our lives to open up space for something deeper, even if it's as simple as turning off the TV to play a board game. Likewise, when we invest in something deep, the shallow stuff can take a backseat, like when dinner with friends means our mobiles all get turned off.

This is not about rules.

Some things tend to make our lives deeper; some make them shallower. It's not a to-do list. We're free to decide how it works for us. Some shallow stuff is necessary, or it saves time for deep things. But the key is to consider carefully how we shape our lives.

What we need most is what Stephen Covey calls "a burning 'yes'":

> Many people simply conclude that they are not disciplined enough. My response to that idea is that it's usually not a discipline problem at all. The problem is more often that the person has not yet sufficiently paid the price to get very clear about what matters most to them. Once you have a

burning "yes" inside you about what's truly important, it's very easy to say "no" to the unimportant.[12]

If we can find the burning yes, saying no will look after itself. Yes to being available to those around us. Yes to being *online* less and *on life* more. Yes to the world outside our windows.

God can do wonderful things with that kind of yes.

In my early twenties I used some inheritance money to buy a digital keyboard. I loved that keyboard. I would shut myself away in my study for hours on end, playing and editing its sounds on the computer, producing my own tracks. It could make every sound under the sun. But though they were pretty realistic, none of the sounds actually had the depth and resonance of a *real* sound. And, of course, I wasn't actually creating any of them.

My guitar is another matter. It takes practice and patience and tuning. It will only ever be one instrument. The B string easily goes flat. It is decorated with dents from sixteen years of use. But pluck just one string on that guitar, and you can feel the note reverberate through the air, filling the guitar body with sound and resonating with other strings so that their harmonies dance off its frequency. I can play the guitar for my kids, or round a fireside, or on the beach.

A while back I had a choice to make. I realized that, whereas Jesus told his disciples to sell their possessions and give to the poor, I hadn't sold a single thing to give money to anyone. So I decided to sell something.

I could choose—the keyboard or the guitar. A thousand instruments or one. Digital perfection or amateur songs.

I sold the keyboard.

I don't miss it.

PART THREE

Adventures in Generosity

CHAPTER 10

▌Idol

Do you know what the financial services industry calls rich people?

High Net Worth Individuals.

This is one of my favourite financial jokes. I suppose the word *rich* can be a little – How can I put this? Embarrassing? Loaded? *High Net Worth* is the financial world's more complimentary alternative.

Me personally, I don't think I've ever met a High Net Worth Individual. It's hard to say though, because I'm not sure how the calculations work.

I've met people who earn lots of money. Does that make them *worth* more than others? I would have thought all people are worth the same.

But even if they do earn plenty, which is not necessarily a bad thing, I still don't get the logic. My accounting isn't what it could be, but I thought that *net* was what you got when you took away what isn't owed elsewhere. In this case, they came into the world with nothing, all they ever had was a gift, and they'll leave with nothing.

That makes a net wealth of zero.

Is that high?

So maybe I've never met a High Net Worth Individual. Or maybe that's the only kind of individual you or I ever meet.

What could keep us from seeing this? Why do we so easily evaluate people in financial terms? How did we come to accept that money really is the bottom line?

III

Money unmasked

Every adventure needs a villain. Sometimes, like on *Scooby Doo* (if you remember the cartoon), the baddy looks like a ghostly monster but turns out to be the old fairground owner who dressed up in a costume because he was bitter about the proposed new housing development – or something like that.

The adventure of generosity has a villain. It isn't money, as such. Money, as we know, can give gifts; it can relieve poverty; it can reward labour. The villain is money's monster name – Mammon. Mammon is the beastly side of money. It's what happens when money gets out of control. Mammon is what money becomes when money protects its own interests.

If we want to transform consumerism, we need to learn how to unmask money and hand it over to the proper authorities (tell me when I'm stretching the Scooby Doo analogy too far).

Money can seem pretty harmless. I mean, in the early days it used to be just shells, for Pete's sake! We keep it in our pockets. It's *our* money. There's barely a cent worldwide that isn't owned or looked after by someone.

And yet we say it makes the world go round.

So when Jesus spoke about money and the dangers of wealth, he called it Mammon. Mammon was a normal Aramaic word for wealth, but Jesus gave it a capital M. According to him, Mammon is like a person in its own right. You may think you've got control of your cash as it lies dormant in your purse or grows quietly in your bank. But Mr Money has a life of his own. If we're not careful, he takes over.

Mammon is money on steroids. It grows more and more powerful. It spills over into areas where it doesn't belong. Marriages implode over it; sex is traded for it; life choices are made in pursuit of it; waking hours are spent dreaming of it. Our money becomes our master.

Spiritually speaking, Mammon is an idol, a God-substitute. In other words, Mammon is what money becomes when it disguises itself as God. Two deities compete for our attention, Jesus claimed. But only one can win. "You cannot serve God and Mammon."

Does this sound unreal? Do people really worship money? Do they sing songs to it or gather weekly in its name?

Not exactly. But money easily assumes godlike status. We turn to it for comfort in the present; we trust it for security in the future. The Mysterious Market governs the big decisions of our nations. Comfort, security, guidance—these are the roles of a deity. The fact is that whatever takes first place in our lives is our god. When money does this, the spiritual implications are huge. Or, as the Bible puts it, "Greed ... is idolatry."[1]

So how do we know if money is our idol?

We could run a personal checklist. Do any of the following apply to you?

- ☐ I become unhappy when I lose money.
- ☐ I envy the lifestyle/possessions of others.
- ☐ I worry about being poor.
- ☐ I measure people by their income/appearance.
- ☐ I evaluate most decisions in financial terms.

We might as well include "I have a heartbeat" or "I hate warts." Men and women, young and old, High and Low Net Worth Individuals—we can all end up thinking in dollar signs.

In fact, even if we can't detect financial idolatry in our lives, that doesn't mean it isn't there. One of the surefire signs of devotion to Mammon is thinking that the love of money isn't an issue for us! Greed's greatest trick is to make us defensive. "Me? Greedy? Surely not. And who are you to judge?!" Besides, we can always find someone superrich who is "worse" than us. Tim Keller observes this brilliantly:

> Money has the power to keep you from asking questions – about how you make your money and how you spend your money. The power of greed is not to ask; the power of greed is not to think; the power of greed is to say, "It's not true of me."[2]

It doesn't work like this for all of us. I'm the opposite, we might say. I see greed everywhere, and I hate it with a passion. Does that mean I've escaped Mammon's clutches?

Probably not. Thrifty budgeteers are just as vulnerable. You don't have to be wealthy to be always thinking about money. Some of us are addicted to money-saving tips, or we're cross that wealthy people are so selfish, or we're obsessed with financial justice. The result is the same: Mammon rules. Everything is still about money. In the words of the biblical proverb, some of us are "always thinking about the cost."[3]

One way or other, whether we barely notice it or spend our energy railing against it, Mammon has a way of positioning itself exactly where it wants to be – at the top of the agenda. That has always been its genius, and it remains the case today. That's why consumerism is so powerful – it is underwritten by the love of money. Mammon is its (unofficial) Official Sponsor. Consumerism is just the latest host culture for Mammon's age-old virus.

When money met its master

Who can help with this? Who has the right to dethrone an idol and the power to return things to their proper perspective?

Ask any question of any child in Sunday school, and you'll have your answer.

Jesus. He came to a world where money was just as much a talking point as it is now. In those days it was questions about dividing inheritances, building barns and storing up possessions (which counted as security, like a savings account). And Jesus devoted a surprising amount of his teaching to it.

His society reflected the classic money polarization too.

On the one hand, many people, threatened by the constraints of living in an occupied land, had made compromises. They collected taxes for the Roman oppressors. Or they sold their bodies to make a living. Or they traded in "unclean" Gentile cities. There were names for these people: prostitutes, tax collectors, sinners. Holy folk steered clear of them, driven by a toxic mix of wounded national pride and repressed envy.

On the other hand, there were the rule bearers. They had a passion for Ethical Living, and they weren't afraid to share it. They vilified the collaborators, condemned the sex workers and insisted on every fine detail of financial law. And in the process they became joyless ambassadors for legalism. They even gave their name to it: the Pharisees. When they got their chance, they implemented the rough justice of a stoning, but mostly they dreamed of revolution.

Are these two sides so different from how it works today?

Some of us make compromises to the market; others throw stones.

Anyway, Jesus walked into that world and utterly transformed it. He lived a third way. A grace-filled transformation. A secret revolution. He welcomed the tax collectors, prostitutes and sinners. He dined at rich men's tables. But he also held out his hands to the legalists, reasoning with them, calling to them. He could debate the Scriptures with the best of them, and he pointed them to a larger mercy, a stranger kingdom than they had dreamed of.[4]

He had a counter-Mammon strategy too. It went like this:

First, Jesus claimed the place of money. Luke is a great guide on this. He gives us a blast of Jesus' teaching in chapter 12 of his gospel:

> "Watch out! Be on your guard against all kinds of greed; life does not consist in an abundance of possessions..."

> "Do not worry about your life, what you will eat; or about your body, what you will wear...."

> "And do not set your heart on what you will eat or drink; do not worry about it. For the pagan world runs after all such things, and your Father knows that you need them. But seek his kingdom, and these things will be given to you as well.

> "Do not be afraid, little flock, for your Father has been pleased to give you the kingdom. Sell your possessions and give to the poor. Provide purses for yourselves that will not wear out, a treasure in heaven that will never fail, where no thief comes near and no moth destroys. For where your treasure is, there your heart will be also."[5]

This is what he's saying: "You want life? You want security? You want a future? Come to me. Let me take money's place. Fix your heart on me and the kingdom I'm bringing. Let that be your treasure. Let it come first. *Everything else* will be taken care of. Call off the chase for more. Sell your possessions—that is, decrease your material security [notice, this is a general instruction given to his disciples]. Give to the poor. Start out with me on an adventure of generosity."

In short—"Lose the idol; follow me."

Second, Jesus overturned money's way of thinking. We've seen how money has a habit of reducing everything to financial figures. In contrast to this, Jesus seemed to make a point of playing with numbers. He subverted the logic of money with the strange arithmetic of grace. A large part of his strategy here was to tell what we could call counter-financial tales:

A group of labourers work different hours, but they all receive the same pay.

A wealthy landowner plans to expand his holdings, but overnight he loses everything.

A penniless widow offers a tiny gift to God, but in the process she outgives the sizeable donations of the great and good.[6]

What's going on?

In God's economy, money isn't just added or subtracted; it multiplies and divides in all kinds of bizarre ways. Grace triumphs over calculation. Love counts more than numbers. It's the odd math of grace. It doesn't add up, and the reason it doesn't add up is that if God ever totalled up our account with him, we'd never get out of minus numbers. So mercy wins the day, and the balance sheet goes out the window.

It was more than a matter of stories, though. The counter-financial tales were matched by counter-financial practices. Give to those who ask of you, and don't expect repayment. Be willing to cancel debts. Decrease your assets for the sake of others.[7]

Can you see what Jesus is doing? He's cutting money down to size. He's refusing to let it set the agenda. He's forcing it to flow in unusual directions, making it the servant of a greater goal.

Weirdly, it's not as if Jesus *needed* the money. He could throw a feast costing more than eight months' wages using only a child's lunch hamper. He could pay his taxes by plucking coins from the mouth of a fish (no, really, a fish! It's like he was being *deliberately* bizarre. He might as well have paid his dues in twigs and berries!).[8]

Jesus even refused to let money set the agenda in a good way. Once, in the week before he died, a woman tenderly anointed him with luxurious perfume fit for a king. However, in the meantime, some of his disciples were already doing the sums.

300 denarii for the perfume = 1 year's wages = a waste

She should have sold the perfume and given the money to the poor. Right?

But they didn't get it, and Jesus had to set them straight. Sometimes even the relief of destitution has to be put in perspective. The kingdom revolution Jesus brings is messy; poverty will always be an issue. And there are things even more important than meeting others' physical needs.[9] In this case, Jesus opts for an act of lavish beauty in his name over the efficient use of cash.

Isn't that interesting?

Jesus invited all sorts of people to sell their possessions and give to the poor. But the one time *someone else* made the suggestion, he wasn't having any of it.

It's like only he has the right to ask people to give something away.

Why only him? Who is he?

It's as if all our things are really his.

Money wins/money loses

So how does this play out in the life of Jesus? Does money always capitulate to his coming?

Luke tells two stories, in chapters 18 and 19. As Jesus heads to Jerusalem for the ultimate adventure in generosity, he meets two rich men along the way.

The first (often called "the rich young man," as we don't know his name) is eager to question Jesus about eternal life. After a polite but frustrating conversation about how good they both are, Jesus cuts to the chase. "You still lack one thing. Sell everything you have and give to the poor, and you will have treasure in heaven. Then come, follow me."

This guy looked blessed. He looked like he had everything. He looked like exactly the kind of person a new movement needs. But Jesus just looked straight into him and said, "You lack."

You lack. But you don't have to lack. Sell everything you have, and you won't lack anymore (more crazy arithmetic).

What happened next? Luke tells us: "When he heard this, he became very sad, because he was a man of great wealth."

The man went away. The idol remained untoppled. Money wins.

Mammon 1   Kingdom of God 0

Now most of the comment I've heard on these verses goes something like this:

> The rich young man had a *particular* problem with money. That's why Jesus asked him to give it up. It was a kind of private therapeutic suggestion between Jesus and him. He just happened to love money *too much*. If he'd been too attached to his rabbits, Jesus would have asked him to give up rabbits. If he'd loved cheeseburgers too much, Jesus would have prescribed a vegan diet. Money was his problem, but it may not be our problem. So the words probably don't apply to us.

Hmmm. Nice try.

I love the way we say, "Jesus only said it to him because the rich man loved money."

Like that's not how we'd respond??!!

Like if he asked me to sell everything and give it to the poor, I'd be so different!

I wouldn't be sad. I'd say, "Only that?! Man, I thought you were going to ask me something difficult! Sell everything? Everything? That's no problem! What about all the money? Oh, let the poor have it. I was just looking after it for them anyway."

The rich young man wasn't some weird wealth junkie who obsessed about the tinkle of tiny coins and the feel of cash on flesh. He was just an ordinary well-to-do guy. Luke doesn't say he went away sad "because he was greedy." No, the sadness was there "because he was a man of great wealth."

There's something about wealth. How can I put this? It makes it hard to enter the kingdom of God. Actually, that's not it exactly. *Giving away* wealth can be a great sign of entering the kingdom. It's *keeping it* that's the problem.[10] There's a saying: "Money swore an oath that nobody who did not love it should ever have it."

Of course, it would be a disaster to reintroduce legalism at this point. Impossible targets, hypocritical condemnations, narrow-minded boundaries between who's "in" and "out." Jesus had no time for any of that. But what if, in our efforts to avoid legalism, we underestimate the subtle perils of wealth?

Money can be dangerous.

It's like scuba diving. If you go scuba diving, the air you breathe at depth keeps you alive. But there's a rule all divers must remember: keep breathing. Inhaling at fifty yards down is vital, but that air is at a different pressure from the air you breathe on the surface. If you keep it in your lungs, it can kill you. So you must keep breathing in and out.

Money is just the same. It is both lifesaving and deadly. We need money to live. But as we come up to the light, we *have* to let it go. We have to be willing to give and receive – to breathe in and out. If we keep holding our money in, it could be the end of us.

The story of the rich young man applies to all of us.

But, in a way, Jesus was wrong.

The rich young man *did* receive eternal life.

He has been immortalized as the man who turned his back on grace.

Money is that powerful – it can keep us from the very thing we've been made to enjoy forever.

But Luke is not finished. There's a second man, Zacchaeus, who was also wealthy. His career choice as a tax collector made him unpopular, but he adjusted to this by taking up an interest in tree climbing (or possibly he was just a Low Net Height Individual). Anyway, the outcome couldn't be more different.

Jesus meets Zacchaeus as he continues his long walk to Jerusalem. He calls Zacchaeus down from his vegetative viewpoint and invites himself over for dinner. But Zacchaeus doesn't wait to be challenged about money. He is ahead of the game. "I give half of my possessions to the poor, and if I have cheated anybody out of anything, I will pay back four times the amount."

Result! Money loses.

Notice, Zacchaeus doesn't give away everything. In a stunning feat of numerical oddity (which we should be used to by now), whereas the rich man was asked for everything, in this case half is somehow OK.

Zacchaeus loses his money but finds his way. "Salvation has come to this house," Jesus announces. And he feasts with Zacchaeus, which is a taste in advance of the banquet God will one day throw for all his people (just like the rich young man's sadness is a foretaste of the destiny he has chosen).

Mammon 1   Kingdom of God 100

(Have you got the hang of the numbers yet?)

Luke wants us to see the contrast between the two rich men. In the first case, money wins, but it doesn't lead to happiness. Like all idols it doesn't deserve its place. We end up the slave.

In the other case, money loses, but Zacchaeus doesn't suffer for it. We last encounter him having dinner with God and launching a process of restitution with his community. The triumph is always greater when the kingdom of love wins.

The invitation

Here comes a crunch point in the Consumer Detox.

At the end of the day it all turns on this: the invitation.

Jesus made an offer to all who met him. If the records we have for his life are even half true, he travelled a great distance to make it and it cost him dearly.

He invites us to grant first place to him and his kingdom. Only this can break us out of the self-centred patterns of consumerism. Only this can release us from the grasp of money.

Now before we go any further, we need to get to something absolutely essential.

This is not about whether we call ourselves "Christians" or not.

You might be reading this right now with your feet up in the Pontifical Lounge of the Vatican (presumably because there's nothing good on TV). You might be on your way home from a meeting of Atheists "R" Us.

"Christian" is a label. It's not that it doesn't matter, but at this stage it's the last thing that's important. What counts at this point is not what we *say* takes the highest place in our lives; what counts is what *actually* takes the highest place.

Jesus was clear that some people would get the words right (call him "Lord, Lord"), but they still wouldn't enter the kingdom. Others came with questions, but they had an instinctive feel for God's priorities. To them he said, "You are not far from the kingdom of God."[11]

Being a "Christian," calling Jesus "Lord," is not the heart of the issue. For many of us, it doesn't actually change the shape of our lives. I have never forgotten the way Tom Sine expressed this:

> In spite of all the talk about Christ's "lordship," everyone knows that the expectations of modern culture come first. Everyone knows that getting ahead in the job comes first. Getting ahead in the suburbs comes first. Getting the children off to their activities comes first. And we tend to make decisions in these areas pretty much like everyone else does, based on our income, our professions, and our social status.
>
> Essentially, most Western Christians unquestioningly allow modern culture to arrange most of the furniture of our lives: forty- to eighty-hour workweeks, single-family detached housing, congested time schedules for our lives and children.[12]

In fact, Jesus predicted that the mundane stuff of life would crowd out his invitation. In Luke 14, he states that the kingdom is like a great banquet that many people are invited to. But one person is distracted by the pressures of work; another is halfway through a shopping trip; one more is busy setting up a home and family. Here's the point: if we're still wrapped up in the pursuits of the surrounding culture, we haven't really accepted the invitation to the kingdom feast.

Some of us may think we've accepted the offer, but in reality we are only toying with it. Ron Sider, who has been a voice for generosity and justice for many years now, writes, "I fear that many – probably most – Western Christians worship the god of materialism."[13]

But there will be others – unlikely candidates for the kingdom – who are actually closer than anyone realizes.

Lose the idol, Jesus says. The proof of this will be in your actions.

There's a second objection that needs to be faced here too.

Why bring God into this? Why get all religious?

Can't consumerism be resisted by just caring for others and the world around us? Why do Jesus and his kingdom have to come first?

Because consumerism is a religious phenomenon. It's not just about shopping and never has been. It's about how we find identity and make meaning. As we've seen, ceaseless consumption is fuelled by a hopeless view of the universe. Only a greater story can bring meaning and purpose.

Consumerism has its shopping mall cathedrals and desire-forming ads. We need spiritual resources for a different way of life.

Consumerism has a power all its own, and because of this, any recovery depends on a higher power (ask Alcoholics Anonymous).

If we cut the Creator out of the picture, and exclude the values of the kingdom of God, there's not much left to help us evaluate the present world order. All we're left with is what you think or what I think. It becomes even easier for some of us to compromise and others to condemn.[14]

But if we commit ourselves to the kingdom story, we have all the resources we need. We have a worldview that tells us why people matter and why creation counts. But it also reminds us that we aren't God, and so we shouldn't take it upon ourselves to judge others. It's a story that has at its heart the love of others at great expense. There is no counter-consumerist narrative like it. And those who find themselves in its scope discover the mysterious presence of God right alongside them.

So the invitation stands. Money can be deposed; a different ordering of our priorities is possible; grace can win the day.

"The kingdom of God is near. Repent and believe the good news!"[15]

|||||||||||||||||||||||||||||||||||||||||||||||||||||||||||||||||||||||||||||||||||||||||||

Dethroning money

How do we kick money where it hurts?

Easy. Idols feed on worship; rulers thrive on the respect of those they govern. But what if instead of worshiping money, we profane it? What if we refuse to pay our dues to Mammon?

In the words of Richard Foster:

> We need to find ways to shout no to the god money. We must dethrone it...
>
> So step on it. Yell at it. Laugh at it. List it way down on the scale of values.... And engage in the most profane act of all—give it away. The powers that energize money cannot abide that most unnatural of acts, giving.[16]

How can we implement this incendiary advice? We could begin by grabbing money by the scruff of the neck and learning how to budget.

Budgeting helps us face up to any debts we owe and to accept a new responsibility for our financial choices.

We can resist money's rule by deliberately downsizing or reducing our assets or giving a proportion of our income away. Ten percent may be a good place to start (but don't tell the rich young man I suggested that!).

We can refuse to let money set the agenda. Time is not money. We are *all* High Net Worth Individuals—not because of what we have but because of the One who values us. The bottom line is not the bottom line.

We can show money who's boss. That is, we can use it to point to the real Boss. Our transactions and the way we make them can become signs of the kingdom that is coming. Works of art dedicated to the King.

I've begun to attempt this.

I'm trying to give in some way to everyone who asks me in the street (whether they look deserving or not).

I've begun to give away books from my library rather than lending them.

An artist friend of mine once offered to create a unique piece for Ailsa and me—something to capture the way God has held us through the stormiest moments of our lives. Initially I was unsure. Even at mate's rates, it wasn't the sort of expenditure I'd usually make. But then I reconsidered. I chose to depart from the script; I chose beauty over economy. And I'm so glad that I did. A beguiling, serene painting now takes pride of place in our bedroom. It is the one possession of significant value that we have.

I try to treat checkout girls like princesses.

Small things. A messy revolution. Pointers to a different kingdom. Signs of the unravelling of Mammon's rule.

In the office where I work, we usually take turns buying drinks for a refreshment break (usually cans of drink, maybe a snack). One time, when it was my turn to take the orders, a colleague joked, "I'll have a bottle of Chablis!"

Cheeky.

I went out and bought him the best vintage Chablis I could find.

The rules of office politeness didn't require it.

On that occasion, I rather broke my budget.

But there are many things more important than money.

Anyway, who's counting?

CHAPTER 11

▌Openhanded

I remember my student days well.

I don't think I've ever lived with such spontaneity, thrift, humour, industry and laziness – all at the same time.

Almost everything was bargain basement, patched together, improvised.

Some nights, in our student house, we would sit in the tiny backyard drinking impossibly cheap French wine called Fin du Vin. "Fin du Vin," we said, "must mean fine wine!" At that price, though, it probably meant final dregs of the vintage.

We played ridiculous jokes on each other. One night some girls came over to trash our house while we were out. When they got to my room, they couldn't tell if they'd already trashed it or not.

We took stuff lightly because we didn't own it.

OK, some of this was irresponsible. The less said about "Indoor Soccer Until We Smash The Lightbulb" the better.

But in a way we were free. We profaned money and value. We got by on pasta. We prioritized relationships, fun and the occasional trip to the library.

So what changed?

What happened to our carefree existence?

What happened to not worrying about how everything looks?

You could say we grew up. In a sense that's true. We began to own things. We no longer lived at our parents' expense. We became the kind of people others could rely on.

But I can't help feeling that something has been lost.

Our growing list of possessions has given us an ever-rising sense of expectation. I can barely imagine living with some of the compromises I once made. I'm amazed we didn't die of food poisoning, for starters. That's the point though – we didn't. We survived. We thrived.

But now a door has closed on that way of life, just as our hands – now full of possessions and responsibilities – have closed in on what we have. We have become the next generation of leading consumers, and the freedom of those student days just feels like a dream.

But it doesn't have to be like this.

The biblical book of Deuteronomy captures the alternative with beautiful simplicity:

> If anyone is poor among your people in any of the towns of the land that the LORD your God is giving you, do not be hardhearted or tightfisted toward them. Rather, be openhanded and freely lend them whatever they need.[1]

Be openhanded. Hold loosely what you have and freely release it to others. This isn't just an attitude for carefree teenagers. It's a whole approach to life.

So how do we open our hands?

||||||||||||||||||||||||||||||||||||||||||||||||||||||||||||||||||||||||||||||||||||||

▌Life in a graced universe

The most important question to ask ourselves if we want to be openhanded is: What universe are we living in?

This may sound a bit odd. I mean, if you and I are currently living in different universes, how come you're reading these words? (I feel a sci-fi novel coming on …)

To put it another way, what's the fundamental reality of the world we live in? Is it a harsh, uncaring world where everything is purely random? If that is our belief, a certain way of life will naturally flow from it.

Is the universe governed by inescapable karma or the judgements of a vengeful god? This, too, would lead us to a certain way of life.

Or is there something else at the heart of the universe?

Like grace.

The idea that grace is at the heart of the universe is as radical as edible clothes. It's easily professed but rarely lived. The New Testament author, James, gets right to the heart of it. He wrote to people who struggled to give to others. But he didn't start by telling them off for being stingy. He started by setting out a different view of the universe:

> Every good and perfect gift is from above, coming down from the Father of the heavenly lights, who does not change like shifting shadows.[2]

Every good thing comes from God. This world is full of his faithfully given gifts. If James's readers can get their heads around that fact, then they've taken the first step to openhanded living.

It's the same for us.

We live in a graced universe. But to see it requires a fundamental shift of consciousness. We need a kind of grace awakening. We need the kind of realization that dawned on one of the characters in Vladimir Nabokov's story *Beneficence:*

> I became aware of the world's tenderness, the profound beneficence of all that surrounded me, the blissful bond between me and all creation; and I realized that joy ... breathed around me everywhere, in the speeding street sounds, in the hem of a comically lifted skirt, in the metallic yet tender drone of the wind, in the autumn clouds bloated with rain. I realized that the world does not represent a struggle at all, or a predaceous sequence of chance events, but shimmering bliss, beneficent trepidation, a gift bestowed on us and unappreciated.[3]

This isn't about being a dewy-eyed optimist. It's about sensing that grace is somehow at work in every corner of this world. For all its pains and frustrations, life is still a gift.

And so the first act of an openhanded life is simply this:

Receive.

With every heartbeat we receive the gift of life. But for those who accept the invitation to follow Jesus, there is so much more than just existence.

Our life is given back to us. Our past is wiped clean with a gift of forgiveness, which, according to Jesus, is equivalent to the cancellation of a debt of millions.

We enter a space of loving relationship with the Father, surrounded by his care and company. Effectively, this is the gift of royal status (which is not cheap).

We encounter a world of divine possibility; we taste "the powers of the coming age."[4] And, despite the mess and mistakes, we come to know God's love made real in genuine Christian community. Jesus described this as receiving a hundred times whatever we might have given up for him.

We are granted the privilege of glimpsing the truth. We are honoured with the task of making a difference in this world.

And more than this, beyond present lines of sight, we are given the promise of enjoying and shaping a renewed universe. And we have the guarantee that all the events of our lives, even our most desperate moments, will be dignified with meaning.

If chapter 3 made us rich, these treasures are off the chart! "All things are yours," exclaims Paul at one point to his infuriatingly shortsighted Corinthian friends.[5]

All this is ours to enjoy. It is gratis, a gift on Someone Else's expenses. But it can only be received with open hands. No one drinks from a stream using clenched fists. There's a point we need to reach where we realize that all we can bring to God is our own emptiness.

But in a graced universe, that is enough.

The flow of grace

Life can be a pretty selfish business (and I'm not just thinking of family board games). But a look beneath the surface reveals some rather different dynamics. It turns out that grace is not restricted to God. A principle of generosity flows through creation like an electrical current. Grace is scattered liberally all over the place. Which is fitting, I guess.

Consider the Pacific salmon.

After a few years in the open ocean, Pacific salmon return to their place of birth to spawn. Somehow they manage to navigate their way back, a journey of over a thousand miles, to the river of their origin (often somewhere along the western coast of North America). The returning salmon must then battle their way up the river, past grizzly bears and over waterfalls, in some cases swimming upstream for another two thousand miles.

As if that wasn't enough, mature Pacific salmon can't tolerate fresh water. As soon as they reenter the river system, their bodies start to shut down. So they complete the entire final leg of this monumental journey without any food. Yet something spurs them on and guides them to the exact stretch of gravel where they themselves were hatched.

When they have lain their eggs, battered, exhausted, their very appearance changed by the fresh water that is literally killing them, the salmon die. To give new life costs them everything.

And then something quite wonderful takes place. As their carcasses decay on the riverbed, they provide nutrients for the eggs to be born into. In more ways than one, they die for their offspring. Life gives itself away for others.[6]

The same principle is at work in your body right now. Whenever your cells find themselves damaged, infected or unnecessary, they can automatically end their life (it's known as *apoptosis*). In this one day, around fifty billion of your cells will purposely self-destruct for the greater health of your whole body. Life gives itself away.

It happens in human relationships too. I discovered this once, quite by chance, in a conversation with my dad. I was worried about becoming a parent, so I asked him: "Dad, why did you do it? How did you put up with all the aggravation we've given you over the years? Didn't it feel like a big sacrifice?"

He replied with one of the Top Five Wisest Things he's ever said. "No," he said, "it wasn't like that at all. It was a joy and a privilege—we *loved* doing it."

That blew me away. Somehow, by the same mysterious principle as the salmon and the cells, the giving had come naturally. This is how it is. The great relational steps we make in life draw us out of self-focus. It's like there's a rightness, even a joy, in acting unselfishly.

Can you see this?

There's a flow of grace at work — a movement away from our selves — and it operates *at every level of the universe*. Of course, not everything follows this flow. Sometimes all we see are glimpses and hints of a deeper pattern. But the pattern is there. Openhandedness is the secret of all reality.

So here's the billion-dollar question (can I use that phrase?): Why is life like this? Why is self-giving at the heart of everything?

It's the Trinity's fault.

The persons of the Trinity love giving. They're always at it. The Father constantly upholds the Son and the Spirit. He gives the Son to the world. The Son offers his life back to the Father. The Spirit pours out his presence on creation.

Give, give, give.

Giving is part of who God is. So when it came to creation, God patterned giving into the very heart of it. Like an Italian chef with olive oil, he couldn't help adding his favourite ingredient. Like an invoice from a mechanic, his fingerprints are all over it.

This is why life works as it does. Or why it doesn't work. There's a flow of grace, and we can no more buck the trend and still live well than we can change the value of pi. Tim Keller explains it like this:

> If you favor money, power, and accomplishment over human relationships, you will dash yourself on the rocks of reality. When Jesus said you must lose yourself in service to find yourself, he was recounting what the Father, Son, and Holy Spirit have been doing throughout eternity. You will, then, never get a sense of self by standing still, as it were, and making everything revolve around your needs and interests. Unless you are willing to experience the loss of options and the individual limitation that comes

from being in committed relationships, you will remain out of touch with your own nature and the nature of things.[7]

True.

This is also how you know if you've found God (or, indeed, if God has found you). It shows. People who walk with God have entered the flow of grace, and it's plain to see. Love is all over them. "Whoever lives in love lives in God," wrote John. Or, as God himself once said about one of his friends, "He defended the cause of the poor and needy.... Is that not what it means to know me?"[8]

I guess God should know.

The gift of giving

This may not be something we're used to.

Some of us treasure our independence. We don't give to others because we fear there won't be enough. Or we don't like to receive because it makes us dependent on others' generosity.

But giving is by far the best way to live: not grasping or controlling; not clinging to our rights or fistfighting for our ambitions. Openhandedness is the soul's true shape. As Eugene Peterson put it, we were born for this:

> Giving is what we do best. It is the air into which we were born. It is the action that was designed into us before our birth.... Some of us try desperately to hold on to ourselves, to live for ourselves. We look so bedraggled and pathetic doing it, hanging on to the dead branch of a bank account for dear life, afraid to risk ourselves on the untried wings of giving. We don't think we can live generously because we have never tried. But the sooner we start the better, for we are going to have to give up our lives finally, and the longer we wait the less time we have for the soaring and swooping life of grace.[9]

What we've uncovered here is the secret of grace. In the words of the

Master: "it is more blessed to give than to receive." Or, as the
put it, there's a "grace of giving" – literally a *gift* of giving.[10]

This gives us another paradox to add to the collection. Light bet
both as a particle and a wave (apparently). Men always give better
directions than women, but if they get it wrong, it's the map's fault. No
matter how full I feel there's always room for chocolate. And to give to
others is actually a gift. As the poet Edward Arlington Robinson put it,
"There are … two kinds of gratitude: the sudden kind we feel for what we
take, the larger kind we feel for what we give."[11]

This doesn't mean that all our efforts at being generous will smoothly
succeed. It's not a magical formula. There's mystery at work. It requires
trial and error and a good dose of humble patience. But the truth
remains.

Giving is a gift. Nothing more paradoxical; nothing more true.

My favourite story about this is told in Mike Riddell's excellent book
Godzone:

> A certain woman had a vivid dream. In it she saw a man with untidy long
> hair and bare feet sitting on a bench outside the post office. A voice said
> to her that if she were to ask this man, he would give her something that
> would make her rich forever. She woke and shrugged the dream off. But
> the next day while walking through town, she saw the man from her dream
> sitting on the bench outside the post office. Feeling somewhat foolish,
> she approached the man and explained her dream. He listened, and then
> reached into his rucksack. He produced an enormous gold nugget, saying,
> "I found this beside the road. Here, it's yours if you want it."
>
> She looked longingly at the nugget. It was huge, sufficient to make her
> wealthy. That night she could not sleep, tossing and turning in her bed. At
> dawn she set off to find the tramp, who was sleeping under a tree in the
> park. She woke him and said, "Give me that wealth that makes it possible
> for you to give this treasure away."[12]

◄ The ultimate rhythm of life

I promised I wouldn't do this as a preacher—tell schmaltzy stories about my kids. But I also made the Scout's promise, and look how that's going.

I came downstairs just now, and there's Jonah, our six-year-old, playing at the kitchen sink. He was fiddling with the tap, turning it on and off, and all the time he was holding a spoon underneath the flow. He was lost in fascination as the water splashed off the spoon and all around the basin.

"Look, Daddy," he called me over. My response: "You're not making a mess, are you?" (I'm such a joy-filled, light-touch parent.) He ignored me. "The tap is God, and the spoon is us." I asked what he meant. "God pours his love into us, and then it splats out to everyone around us."

I don't know where he gets it from.

No, really, I don't. But hey, it's good stuff!

When he's older, he'll make a great theologian. Or hydraulics engineer.

The great Reformer Martin Luther said, "Good things flow from Christ and are flowing into us. These good things flow from us on to those who have need of them."[13] Not bad. But I think it misses the word *splat*.

When we give, we enter the flow of grace. We receive; we give. And in giving, we receive again. And so on.

Open hands receive. Open hands give.

The key is a life with rhythm. Sometimes we have plenty; sometimes we don't. We never reach a fixed point of perfection. We never "arrive." We just learn more about giving and receiving. And when we do, we move in time with the heartbeat of the universe. This is the ultimate rhythm of life.

Now here's the rub.

Everything works according to this rhythm of reciprocity. The back-and-forth of giving and receiving is how character grows and friendships are built (self-interested people rarely build good friendships). It's the key to family life, love and marriage. It's the key to healthy society and sustainable living.[14]

Everything works this way. Except consumerism.

Consumerism isn't about giving and receiving; it's about desiring and buying.

This is a monumental clash. The consuming passion of our culture jars with the ultimate rhythm of life. It's like trying to record an orchestral symphony while Jonny the hyperactive child is messing around on the cymbals. It's like tuning Grandpa's pacemaker to the beat of dance music radio.

No wonder consumerism damages our health, our communities and our environment – it is in near total contradiction with the grace that animates the universe.

Something has to give.

We do.

Giving and receiving is the pinnacle of everything we've covered in this book. The openhanded are consumer resistant. They are free to step off the treadmill. Nothing left to prove through shopping or owning or maximizing. They've seen at last that even who they are – their very identity – is a gift.

Giving and receiving is the greatest of life's rhythms. If we nail every other rhythm of life but not this one, we'll never be more than self-centred eco-activists, so focussed on "balancing" our lives that we end up frozen still. Only the adventure of generosity makes lifestyle change truly worth it.

We are left with a fundamental choice: Is Jesus right about giving, or not?

In the words of Martin Luther King, "Every man must decide whether he will walk in the light of creative altruism or the darkness of destructive selfishness."[15]

Cross-shaped

That's it. We've arrived at the very heart of the Detox. But there is still one level deeper we can go.

Where does this end?

What if we do open our hands?

What might happen?

We see it play out in Jesus. If there was ever any doubt that Jesus was God made flesh, just see how he gave. He was a natural. Giving was in his DNA – almost literally! There are few greater signs of divinity than this.

Jesus certainly received plenty from God. Not just because he daily depended on the Father, but in another way too. He came, as his first followers eventually recognized, from heaven – with all its authority and richness and majesty. He knew what it was to be wealthy in every worthwhile sense.

And yet the testimony of the early Christian writers is clear: he "did not consider equality with God something to be used to his own advantage; rather, he made himself nothing." "Though he was rich, yet for your sake he became poor." "Jesus knew that the Father had put all things under his power ... so he ... began to wash his disciples' feet."[16] Equality with God, riches, ultimate power. Jesus had it all. But he gave it away.

Self-giving was just as counterintuitive in those days. The Jewish nation dreamed of an ironfisted Messiah. They yearned for prosperity, prestige and power (and anything else impressive beginning with *p*). But Jesus walked a different path. He said (in effect), "God's enemies will take my life from my outstretched palms."

He was right. That's what can happen to open hands – they get nailed.

This is what love looks like in a broken world. Even God's love. In fact, *especially* God's love. It lays itself open; it meets others at their point of need. It becomes cross-shaped.

In the Trinity, since before time began, God has known love in delightful mutual surrender. But on the soil of a rebel world, that same love took on a new form: a son's willing sacrifice; a father's grief. We could say the cross is the music of God's love transposed into a minor key. Or in the words of C. S. Lewis:

> In self-giving, if anywhere, we touch a rhythm not only of all creation but of all being.... For when [Jesus] was crucified he "did ... in the wild weather of his outlying provinces [what] he had done at home in glory and gladness."[17]

It was Jesus' trust in his Father that led him to this. As he died, he pushed his belief in the generosity of God to the absolute limit. He risked everything on the premise that even the darkest moment in history could be turned by grace into good.

Whenever hands have been opened for others, God can't bear to leave them empty. So it proved here. Where Jesus gave his all, the Father used his Son's generosity as an occasion for a universal outpouring of grace so that really they were giving together to the whole world.

And Jesus? His empty, nailed hands were raised from death, along with the rest of his re-created body. No one ever gave like he gave; and no one has ever been blessed like he was blessed. At least, not yet ...

Now here it gets even more interesting.

The New Testament talks about financial generosity in many places. Its authors had ample opportunity to reenergize the Old Testament concept of giving a tithe (10 percent). But they didn't. Somehow it no longer seemed appropriate. Somehow, the only picture that summed up the generosity we're called to was the freely offered sacrifice of the Messiah.

Three texts are worth a look:

> Large crowds were traveling with Jesus, and turning to them he said: "If anyone comes to me and does not hate father and mother, wife and children, brothers and sisters – yes, even life itself – such a person cannot be my disciple. And whoever does not carry their cross and follow me cannot be my disciple.
>
> "Suppose one of you wants to build a tower. Won't you first sit down and estimate the cost to see if you have enough money to complete it? For if you lay the foundation and are not able to finish it, everyone who sees it will ridicule you, saying, 'This person began to build and wasn't able to finish.'
>
> "Or suppose a king is about to go to war against another king. Won't he first sit down and consider whether he is able with ten thousand men to oppose the one coming against him with twenty thousand? If he is not able, he will send a delegation while the other is still a long way off and will ask for terms of peace. In the same way, those of you who do not give up everything you have cannot be my disciples."[18]

Carry your cross. This is the cost, and there's no way round it. It's absolutely essential. The supreme benefit of following Jesus, like building a great tower or winning a huge victory, will require all kinds of sacrifice. But notice at the end how Jesus brings this to a point: "Give up everything you have" (the words here literally mean "say good-bye to all your possessions/property"). The biting point of discipleship here – the test of whether or not we're committed to the journey – is our willingness to give up what we own. In other words, carrying your cross is about possessions.

Paul develops the same theme:

But since you excel in everything—in faith, in speech, in knowledge, in complete earnestness and in the love we have kindled in you—see that you also excel in this grace of giving.

I am not commanding you, but I want to test the sincerity of your love by comparing it with the earnestness of others. For you know the grace of our Lord Jesus Christ, that though he was rich, yet for your sake he became poor, so that you through his poverty might become rich.[19]

Excel in giving, he says. And the model and measure of your giving should be the sacrifice of Jesus. He made the poor rich. He minimized himself to maximize others. Now apply that to your finances.

And here's John:

This is how we know what love is: Jesus Christ laid down his life for us. And we ought to lay down our lives for one another. If any one of you has material possessions and sees a brother or sister in need but has no pity on them, how can the love of God be in you? Dear children, let us not love with words or tongue but with actions and in truth.[20]

Jesus laid down his life for us; now we should lay down our lives. We should die for each other (could he have put this any stronger?). "The love of God," operating through us, will make us cross-shaped. And how does this hit the ground? Possessions. Again.

And please, writes John, don't turn this into mere sentiment (loving "with words"). God's love is known and proved in real relationships. It can't just be imbibed by chemical infusion from heaven or received remotely through Christian broadcasting. The love of God comes alive in sacrificial Christian community or it barely lives at all.

This is uncompromising stuff. When it comes to giving, we're not invited into a pattern of percentages. We are not being asked to be "extra generous." We are called to the cross. We are called to a kind of financial death, so that new life might result. This call is not always heard in the church. But God is obviously keen on it, as we can see. He might as well have faxed it to each of us in triplicate!

This doesn't mean that God is looking for us to give *instead* of receiving. But to *truly receive* the cross is to be drawn into its flow of giving. It turns out that the cross is not a Get Out of Jail Free card that costs us nothing at any point. It's more like the gift of a pet. (No one who is given a dog says, "Thank you! Presumably he won't need feeding.") Being a gift doesn't stop it from making demands.

Are you tempted to complain about this? I am. We could submit a complaint together. How could God ask us to give like this?!

But he might respond with a simple question: Which is more blessed – to give or to receive? If Jesus is right, it's the first one. So we are complaining that God is giving us an opportunity to be blessed? Hmmm.

Why would we be scared of being cross-shaped?

Don't we know what happened to the one who bore the scars?

❚ ** Health warning **

At this point many great spiritual writers issue a health warning. Or perhaps it's an unhealth warning. There's an aspect of the human psyche that likes giving things up. Part of us actually *enjoys* playing the martyr.

Some of us love to hate ourselves, and we seek refuge in the invisibility of endless service. Some of us crave the attention of heroism (Christian authors are the worst!). Some of us thrill at tough spiritual talk. Or we know just who needs to hear it.

But none of this is death to self; it's simply another form of self-centredness. True death to self is the end of all harsh criticism (of self and others). No more conceited spiritual athletics. No more obsessional self-pity. Instead, there is a resurrection. A new self is being formed – drenched in grace from head to toe and marked by the freedom that comes from surrendering control.

True generosity isn't about trying harder; it's about letting go. If it feels like torture, we're doing it wrong. The adventure of generosity is just that – an adventure. We take bold, fearful risks, giving beyond what we thought possible, and along the way our faith is enlarged. Then we can take bigger risks. And so it goes on. Looking for the right move at the right time; listening for the Spirit's whispers; learning to flow with the heart of God.

Richard Foster calls this being *simple* instead of just being *sincere*. I see this in myself:

> The sincere are not yet simple. They have a kind of artificial rigor that makes us feel uncomfortable, though we cannot fault the virtue. They put us on edge and make us feel ill at ease.... In reality, however, it is due to the fact that these deeply committed folk are trying too hard. They lack the ease, freedom, and naturalness that mark true interior simplicity....
>
> Actually this reality is not something we can bring about by gritting our teeth and fortifying our will.... Joy, not grit, is the hallmark of holy obedience. We need to be lighthearted in what we do to avoid taking ourselves too seriously. It is a cheerful revolt against self and pride. Our work is jubilant, carefree, merry.[21]

He's right. This isn't a seriousness contest. We need to be openhanded about being openhanded. Joy is the hallmark of a simple life.

Ha ha ha.

Does that do it?

OK, maybe I have a way to go yet.

||||||||||||||||||||||||||||||||||||||||||||||||||||||||||||||||||||||||

▌Adventures past

So what does this look like?

Luke gives us an openhanded history of the early church:

> All the believers were one in heart and mind. No one claimed that any
> of their possessions was their own, but they shared everything they had.
> With great power the apostles continued to testify to the resurrection of
> the Lord Jesus. And God's grace was so powerfully at work in them all that
> there were no needy persons among them. For from time to time those
> who owned land or houses sold them, brought the money from the sales
> and put it at the apostles' feet, and it was distributed to anyone who had
> need.[22]

Full-on sharing – powerful stuff. But this isn't enforced communism. Luke
explains that it's because "God's grace was so powerfully at work."

A century or so later a defender of Christianity, Aristides, shows how this
habit of radical sharing was alive and well in the church:

> He who has gives to him who has not, without boasting. And when they
> see a stranger, they take him in to their homes and rejoice over him as a
> brother.... And if there is among them any that is poor and needy, and if
> they have no spare food, they fast two or three days in order to supply to
> the needy their lack of food.[23]

That really hit me when I first heard about it. They didn't just give their
spare food; they fasted for each other. If this sounds unreal, it's worth
knowing that even the critics of Christianity, like the outspokenly cynical
Lucian, agree that the church was like this:

> The poor wretches have convinced themselves, first and foremost, that
> they are going to be immortal and live for all time, in consequence of
> which they despise death.... Furthermore, their first lawgiver persuaded
> them that they are all brothers of one another.... Therefore they [consider]
> all things ... common property.[24]

Obviously this incredible openhandedness wasn't without dangers. But the point is that they went on a journey, mistakes and all. And many of those who looked on saw that some kind of grace earthquake had impacted history. What else could explain such radical generosity?

None of these accounts are absolute blueprints for the church. The first disciples and these early believers worked out how to express grace differently.[25] Still, something incredible was going on in those early days that looked like divine love in action.

The question is: What would that look like now?

Adventures present

There must be as many ways to be openhanded as there are people (there are plenty of ideas in the Detox Diary at the back of this book). For five years now in the Breathe network we've been collecting stories of what this could look like today.

Real stories, simple acts. Ordinary people with God's extraordinary grace working through them.

Some of them cut the hours of their lucrative city jobs to serve their local church.

Some of them banded together to provide for a family where the breadwinner had been laid off.

Some, finding themselves single, cut back on carefree city life to help foster a child.

Some of them found creative ways to share housing.

Some opened their homes to asylum seekers.

They give. They give increasing proportions of their income. Or second homes. Or their skills to help local charities.

They sacrifice. They give up mobility to commit to a local area. They surrender business-class seats to raise money for others. They sleep their children in shared rooms to make space for hospitality.

They move. From the suburbs to housing estates. From rich Western nations to the ends of the earth. And back again, from time to time.

Open hands.

Open homes.

Open hearts.

Sacrifices that bring life. Adventures in generosity that are only just beginning.

We can join them. We can open our hands.

How come? Only because we have this personal assurance: God is able to give us more than could ever be taken away.

CHAPTER 12

Tele-vision

I love the film *Gladiator*.

It's an epic tale. Trusted general is betrayed by murderous young emperor; ex-general becomes top gladiator; gladiator returns incognito to Rome to confront his enemy and rescue the dream of freedom. Classic.

I remember walking out of the cinema floating on the soaring chords of its closing song. I felt ten feet tall. I was saying Russell Crowe's lines to myself:

> My name is Maximus Decimus Meridius, commander of the Armies of the North, General of the Felix Legions, loyal servant to the true emperor, Marcus Aurelius. Father to a murdered son, husband to a murdered wife. And I will have my vengeance, in this life or the next.[1]

OK, in my case it's more like: My name is Marcus Powlius, employee of a local church, wearer of wannabe surfer gear, owner of a Toyota Corolla Verso. Father to middle-class kids, husband of a middle-class wife. And I will have my popcorn in this film or the next.

Anyway, I was deeply moved. It's a movie about courage. Its promotional taglines were things like "The Gladiator Who Defied an Empire" and "What We Do in Life Echoes in Eternity."

But then, like all films, the credits come up. As I blinkingly accustom myself to the light, I look around and see others moving stiffly back to their cars. I imagine they're having a similar experience—stirred to greatness, inspired to noble fortitude. And I wonder: What difference is tonight's movie really going to make?

Before long, I'm in the car park, and the tears I manfully suppressed (well, nearly) have turned to satisfied sighs. We drive home. Maybe I replay the film in my head or watch the news and go to bed. The next day is much the same as any other.

I've started to wonder: Why don't movies change us?

Why doesn't the glow last?

Why doesn't the heroism rub off?

Far vision

There's something about the experience of watching a movie that is destined to leave us unchanged. But we need to do some creative thinking to uncover it.

Television is an odd word – half Greek, half Latin. The Latin *visio* means "seeing." The Greek *tele* means "far." TV is *far vision* – it brings us images from a distance.

The name is apt. TV can be great entertainment, but it is far removed from us in more ways than one. Distant news items, fictional characters, idealized products. So many images, so far out of reach.

This is why *Gladiator* doesn't change me. There's no true connection with where I'm at. The characters have no commitment to me. They're pure fiction. Russell Crowe doesn't know me. There's no local support group where I can take my response to the film further.

"Mark," you might think, "get a grip. It's just a film."

But that's my point. It's just images on a screen a long way from the realities of my life. And I am just a consumer, a voyeur, chewing through my pick-and-mix sweet selection. OK, some films are truly powerful. But by and large, movies can't bring change at the deepest level.

If I am to be transformed, I need something more.

||||||||||||||||||||||||||||||||||||||||||||||||||||||||||||||||||||||||||||||||

Future vision

Call me a geek (you wouldn't be the first), but we need to do a bit more digging.

Most of the time, *tele* means "far." But there is another possible use of *tele*. It can pick up a different set of Greek words, like *teleios* (meaning "mature" or "completed") and *telos* (meaning "end" or "fulfilment"). These words point forward to the future of things, to their goal. *Tele* can, and occasionally does, refer to this.[2]

So what if we gave the word *television* a different meaning?

Not "far vision" – "future vision."

Vision can take a different meaning too. It can be more than just sight or a picture on a screen:

Vision (noun)
- an image conjured up vividly in the imagination
- the ability to perceive what is likely, and plan wisely for it
- an image communicated supernaturally, especially by God
- someone or something of overwhelming beauty[3]

Isn't that interesting? As it happens, this is pretty much exactly what Jesus came to bring. The kingdom of God, as he called it, is tele-vision (future vision) in this larger sense. It is a coming reality of overwhelming beauty, brought supernaturally by God, to capture our imagination and change our plans.

The kingdom is the vision of God. It's his long-dreamed intention for the world he created. Jesus came to bring it to reality. He instigated it, demonstrated it and gave his life to make it possible.

The kingdom is *tele-vision* in the best possible sense. And it's the key to real transformation.

How does it work?

▌Tales from a place called the future

The kingdom begins with a future.

It begins with what is not yet here (which is why its prayer is "let your kingdom come").

Like a complicated thriller, the kingdom begins with the end. Jesus was consumed by the fulfilled vision of God. He told tales from a place called the future.

What will this future look like? Two things: restoration and reversal.

Restoration – because the world will be put right. There will be a banquet, a party of global proportions: "People will come from east and west and north and south, and will take their places at the feast in the kingdom of God." There will be a "renewal of all things" where every kind of brokenness is swallowed up by an abundant new creation. There will be a judgement where the secrets of history are uncovered and an unfathomable mercy will be poured out.[4]

Jesus fully expected this with every fibre of his being. He never stopped pointing to it, never gave up hope of it. But there was something else as well.

Reversal – because the coming restoration will turn things upside down. "The first will be last." Those the world favours – the wealthy, the winners, the self-satisfied, the dealmakers, those who look after number one – they'll miss out. Instead, Jesus announced an alternative guest list: the poor, the humble, the mercy givers, the peacemakers and those who suffer to bring about justice.

How could life's winners possibly miss out on God's blessing?

Easy – they're not interested. They are too busy constructing their own private paradises. To them, the invitation of the kingdom looks like junk mail, a waste of precious time. This is unfortunate. Imagine a man who has everything, Jesus said – the latest fashions and the finest food. But outside his securely gated residence lies a desperate beggar. In the end it will be the beggar who receives the riches of the kingdom, while the ex-rich man smoulders with envy.[5]

The vision of God will come to pass, and with it a great reversal.

Jesus invested his all in this message. And we see in his life something quite remarkable: it starts coming true around him. By the Power at work within him, he brought the future forward. As he put it, "The kingdom of God is near." So in the gospels we see signs of God's vision all over the place. There's restoration: healings, forgiveness, feasting. And there are reversals too: the poor are blessed; the rich are humbled; religious experts miss the plot; fishermen and female disciples (which was unheard of) take their place.

What's happening? The vision is becoming real; the future is breaking into the present.

Interactive TV

This lands us in a rather unique place. Technically speaking, we currently live in the time after the past event that brought the future into the present!

In other words, God's vision is on its way. The kingdom is coming. Unstoppably.

So, if we're willing, we too can live for it. The vision of God is becoming reality in the middle of a broken world, and we can be part of it.

This is much better news than consumerism. Unlike the tantalizing images of advertising, God's future vision is not out of reach, ever-promising and never delivering. The world has been stirring with hope for two thousand years, and already the restorations and reversals have begun.

Not only that, but unlike the market economy, the kingdom is not exclusive. Anyone is welcome. The cost of admission is only a word.

Yes.

This is the true interactive tele-vision. We can take part in it right now. No remote required. It begins as we let God reverse and restore our lives. Then it ripples out to the world around us.

We can't construct God's kingdom (it's not made "by human hands"[6]). But in a broken world we can provide glimpses of what's coming. We can be signs of the strange new world on its way, interpreters of the joyful secret of history, ambassadors of a future kingdom.

We can dedicate our lives to this vision.

We can speak out for it.

We can invite people to join it.

We can demonstrate it in tiny gestures.

We can pursue it through international policies.

We can stand up for its values, against the ways consumerism distorts society.[7]

Even our daily spending can be part of this. We may not realize it, but every note or coin in our possession serves another vital function: it's also a vote. Every purchase we make sends a signal to the market. The economy, being a thoughtless beast, will follow where demand leads. Where we buy, there's profit. Where we invest, there's growth. So what kind of world do we want to invest in? Do we want to reward cheap, short-lived manufacturing, or sustainable production that makes things to last? Do we want to give our business to companies with poor human rights records, or to those who trade and pay fairly? Consumer spending can work wonders when it is harnessed to the values of God's kingdom.[8]

However we get involved, this is the greatest privilege we can ever have – to allow shafts of kingdom light to stream from the future into our world, like early rays of the new dawn.

Each of us will reflect that light differently.

Some of us will save lives threatened by diseases or disaster. Others will invest in the long-term development of poorer countries.

Some of us will get personally involved with the excluded and desperate. Others will generate huge financial resources or political pressure to change the shape of society.

For some it will be a daily job; for others a passionate pastime. For some it will look impressive (you may take bigger steps than you ever imagined); others may look more ordinary. It's not a competition ("my humble sacrifice is bigger than your humble sacrifice"). We each have a different God-given shape and calling.

The question is: What will it be for you?

❚ The deadline

One day what really matters will become clear. One day there will be no doubt that investing in God's kingdom was by far the wisest move to make.

But Jesus speaks to us now, ahead of time. He tells us how it's all going to unfold. This is our heads-up.

The problem with God-people, though, said Jesus, is they're too nice. When it comes to finances, for instance, they go all woolly-minded. Does it really matter what I do with my money? How much can I keep? I suppose I could try to give a bit here and there – is that enough?

I wish they were more profit driven, said Jesus. (He did! He basically said all this in Luke 16.) I wish God-people ("the children of the light") were shrewd and sharp and knew that a deadline is coming which will change everything.

It's like this: imagine a financial manager in a big-city firm is told he's going to be fired. Quickly, he realizes that without a job he's in big trouble. He says to himself, "I'm too weak for manual labour, and I'm ashamed to beg" – I like him already.

But then he has a brain wave.

There's still time. He's still got his boss's business documents. There is a small window of opportunity, and if he plays his cards right, he can use the company's funds to smooth his way into a better future. So he calls in a few of the firm's major clients. "We're doing a bit of financial restructuring," he bluffs. "I've put in a good word for you with the board, and they've decided to cut your debts by 50 percent. If you just sign here …"

They don't know this guy is on his way out. They don't know he's just making it up as he goes along. Who knows what they think? But we do know that when he calls round at their office next week, with his puppy-dog, newly unemployed face on, he'll get more than a cup of coffee.

That, said Jesus, is what we should all be like when it comes to the kingdom of God. We should think smart. We know the deadline is coming. We only have so long to make use of the finances we have (and, as in the parable in Luke 16, they're not ours anyway!).

The more of the Boss's money we can give away, the better.

Now don't say "that manager broke the rules." Jesus (the "meek and mild" one) told this story without scruples. Of course the manager broke the rules. That's the point. The kingdom breaks the rules. The poor are blessed; the first are last. Deal with it.

If you think about it, what's great about the manager is that he spots what is really going on. He realizes that just keeping his head down and playing by the system's rules won't work. Even if he wins Employee of the Week, it won't save him now. The only thing left is to think outside the box. He has to be counterintuitive: cancel debts, give to others, ignore the usual protocols (can you see what Jesus is doing here?). The best thing the manager can do is invest in the future, because what's coming is irreversible.

▌Risk and reward

Jesus made this point again and again: we need to act counterintuitively for a future reward. At this point, though, we might ask: Isn't it selfish to live for a future reward? Is Jesus trying to bribe us to be nice?

Good question.

I'm tempted to say: if you're not motivated by wealth, that's fine. In that case, you won't need to hold on to the wealth you have. So if you want reward – give; if you don't care about money – give. Generosity wins, either way!

But the answer is deeper than that. There's a sense in which present financial riches are held to the exclusion of others. That's why we keep them behind bars. But kingdom wealth is not like that. Kingdom wealth comes from making other people rich—from giving and sharing.

Why *wouldn't* we want a wealth that comes from making other people rich?

Why wouldn't God want us to pursue that?

Where does that leave us? There's no need to get back into the calculations and neuroses that accompany the idolatry of money. There's no need to collapse into guilt ("what if I don't maximize my kingdom investment?"). Jesus is giving us an invitation to risk and reward. He's calling us to throw ourselves more fully into the rhythm of giving and receiving.

It's all about taking an opportunity.

This happened to me once. I was trekking round Europe and found myself in Zurich's rail station late one night on my way out of Switzerland. I had some Swiss francs to spare, so as my train was getting ready to leave, I wandered over to the shop to buy some chocolate. I made my purchase (Maltesers—surely the best way to enjoy chocolate), I received my change, and off I went.

Only as I walked back to the platform did I realize what a fool I'd been. What was I doing with change? I wasn't going to come back to Switzerland any time soon. Why hadn't I spent everything? What possible use would I have for a random collection of paper and metal that no other country used as currency?

I sprinted back to the counter. "Give me all the Maltesers this money can buy!"

Now there's wisdom. If I'd lived earlier in history, maybe I'd have got to star in a parable …

We should treat all our money like this.

We have money for a limited time. While it's at our disposal we should put it to the best use we can. The more we invest in the restorations and reversals of the kingdom of God the better. Richard Foster is right on the money (so to speak):

> The proper use of money is not for living high down here; that would be a very poor investment indeed. No, the proper use of money is for investing as much of it as possible in the lives of people, so that we will have treasure in heaven. Of course, we need to keep a certain amount of money in order to carry on the day-to-day business of life, but we want to free up as much as we possibly can in order to place it where the return is eternal.[9]

This applies to every action for God's vision. Every injustice righted, every person fed, every possession shared—all this is kingdom investment. As with most investments, there are returns we'll see now and some we'll see later. But the main point is clear: present wealth cannot last; kingdom wealth cannot cease.

Which means the big question isn't "What can I keep?" but "How much can I invest?"

|||||||||||||||||||||||||||||||||||||||||||||||||||||||||||||||||||||||||||||||||||||||||

The cause

Consumerism likes to call itself radical names.

We have sports shoes called things like Passion and Fire and Revolution. But they're not. Really, they just aren't. They're cushioned activity shoes. Canvas stuck on foam. They're not radical at all. Even the luminous ones. They're tame. We've just become so used to the ridiculously overstated language that it washes over us.

We watch movies about heroes. But our lives are pretty unheroic.

I remember the teenage dreams I used to have. I longed for a sports car, a flashy apartment, a string of attractive girlfriends. Actually, just one girlfriend would have been nice. I basically wanted a one-way ticket to Successville.

OK, maybe now the dreams are more refined. Progress at work, a relaxing home, weekend fun, holiday breaks. But how easily we get drawn into the "quiet life" of Radiohead's song "No Surprises":

> A heart that's full up like a landfill,
> a job that slowly kills you,
> bruises that won't heal.
> You look so tired-unhappy,
> bring down the government,
> they don't, they don't speak for us.
> I'll take a quiet life,
> a handshake, some carbon monoxide,
> no alarms and no surprises,
> no alarms and no surprises,
> no alarms and no surprises,
> Silent
> Silent
> This is my final fit,
> my final bellyache,
> with no alarms and no surprises,
> no alarms and no surprises,
> no alarms and no surprises please.
> Such a pretty house
> and such a pretty garden.
> No alarms and no surprises (get me outta here),
> no alarms and no surprises (get me outta here),
> no alarms and no surprises, please.[10]

The job, the house, the garden—and without knowing it, the spontaneity and risk have drained out of our lives. But we have running shoes called Hurricane.

Despite the heroic bluster of advertising copy, consumerism is actually a rather stingy affair. All it asks of us is this: to do whatever we want for as long as we feel like doing it, and not a minute more. As Vincent Miller puts it, "It is, in the end, surprisingly parsimonious, unfamiliar with any splendid expenditure, and reckless, gracious bestowal of one's life."[11]

The kingdom of God is so different. Feed the hungry; open your home; embrace the concerns of the needy. That's truly radical. It's risky and unpredictable, time-consuming and costly.

It's not the quiet life of consumer choices; it's a cause.

The kingdom promises us the world, but it asks us to surrender everything. It's the journey of a lifetime at the cost of a life.

Is that bad news? Maybe not. As Stanley Hauerwas has said, "God has not promised us safety, but participation in an adventure called the kingdom. That seems to me to be very good news in a world that is quite literally dying of boredom."[12]

I saw this in my sister a few years back.

There was a time when I fell out of touch with Sarah. I hadn't been great at staying in contact. She'd been preoccupied with her city job, busy life and boyfriend. God was still on her horizon, but church had dropped down on her list of priorities.

Then gradually there was a stirring in her, and one day I got this amazing email. Sarah had been on a trip, but not as a tourist. She'd spent a few weeks in South America on a farm with children affected by HIV/AIDs. Her time there had made her see through new eyes. She'd been struck by the majesty of the Brazilian mountains and floored by the humility of the woman leading the children's home. Creation, compassion – a bigger vision than she had been living for. And something changed.

"I've written a poem about poverty," the email read.

A poem? A poem?! We barely keep in contact through the year and now my sister is sending me verse! Oh yes. And some poem:

Have our eyes been shut for so long
That we cannot see the truth.
The tears flow inside of me,
but is there enough compassion to wash the world clean?

What had happened to my sister?

She had found a cause. She had been on an adventure of generosity—sacrificial, stretching and totally unconsumerist. After that, there was no stopping her. She had seen something on that trip. The people who give names to running shoes wouldn't know what it was, even if they used a dictionary.

This is where the power of transformation lies—in the vision, in the cause. We may think that being "simple" means shrinking down to a reduced life. But actually the opposite is true.

Simplicity isn't about getting by on "what you need" instead of having "what you want" (such a hard distinction to make anyway); simplicity is about *wanting something else.*

We're not being asked to limit our desire; we're being asked to tether our desire to the wild vision of God.

The truly restricted life is the one focussed on "my preferences, my rights, my potential." The kingdom cause exposes this as narrow, self-obsessed, and dull. In a speech given in June 1963, Martin Luther King Jr. said, "I submit to you that if a man hasn't discovered something he will die for, he isn't fit to live." Half the time consumerism isn't even worth shopping for.

In other words, simplicity isn't having a smaller life; it's having a bigger vision.

▌Keeping the vision alive

But we're not going to end with the big vision.

We're going to end with what keeps the vision alive.

How does the vision get fleshed out?

Four things: story, power, community, symbol.

The Bible is the *story* of the vision. We need the Scriptures to incubate the vision and keep the kingdom conspiracy alive. We can try our best to domesticate its teaching and smother its call for an alternative lifestyle. But Scripture's words are seeds. They grow even through concrete.

The Spirit of God is the *power* of the vision. He initiates us into the rhythms of life. He saves us from the tyranny of our own efforts. Even when change seems hard to come by, we needn't despair. The wind of the Spirit is blowing.

Church is the *community* of the vision. In every generation, God calls his people to be the epicentre of a grace earthquake – restoring lives, reversing fortunes, living out the free economics of the kingdom.

So church should buck the consumer trend. It needs to relate to consumer culture, but it cannot afford to let consumerism into its heart. The minute church becomes a rock concert or an out-of-town superstore, we've lost our way.

We have a lot to learn. But we know one thing already: we cannot make this journey alone. Mike Riddell is right:

> In tackling materialism, there is no way in which this can be addressed by individuals. To live a lifestyle contrary to that of all around is psychologically very difficult for a person on their own. Resistance requires the power and support of a group, who are putting themselves on the

line in solidarity. Only in a group can we begin to hear and respond to the searching words of Jesus on possessions and how they affect us.[13]

So what does this look like?

How do we tackle consumerism together?

You tell me.

Read this book with others. Give it to friends. Try the Detox Diary together. Check out the Breathe network (*www.breathenetwork.org*). Discuss. Experiment. Give God space to bring it all to life.

Community is key. And community is the setting for the symbol of the vision, which is the closest we have to an antidote to Hollywood.

The *symbol* of the vision is something deep – a meal with ingredients that have matured over time. It tells the tale of liberation. It is received by the openhanded. It anticipates the final banquet.

What is the symbol?

Bread broken. Wine poured. "Do this in remembrance of me."

The Lord's Supper is not sexy. It wouldn't look great on a promotional video. Sometimes it is highly charged; sometimes not. There are no sponsors. The un-airbrushed are welcome.

But this simple meal changes us. If we let God go to work.

Why?

Because it is rooted in a real event. Jesus of Nazareth really died on a cross with forgiveness on his lips. God's heart really was broken. For us.

Because sharing bread and wine is a lifestyle. It pulls us out of noncommittal spectating and conscripts us to the kingdom cause.

And because this love feast cuts to the heart of our selfishness with a gift of pure grace.

Gladiator surrenders. Consumerism concedes. As Catholic writer William T. Cavanaugh puts it, "To consume the Eucharist is an act of anti-consumption."[14]

The parallel culture

None of this removes us from the challenges of consumer culture. Occasionally it feels like we spill out of church into car parks, just the same as we do after a movie.

But we shouldn't underestimate the power of these tools. Together they create what has been called a "parallel culture."

In the 1960s, Václav Havel was a playwright in communist Czechoslovakia. His passion for human rights challenged the authorities, who banned his work and imprisoned him several times. But Havel continued to speak out for a different system. Eventually he played his part in the fall of Communism and later became the first president of the Czech Republic.

Havel once described how dissidents under communist rule developed a "parallel culture" to sustain them in their resistance. They told stories; they studied philosophy; they wrote songs. Under the radar of the ruling powers, a different culture was being born. Havel spoke about it like this: "It was impossible for us to live totally outside the system. You cannot live outside a culture. But you can create within it zones and spaces where you can become who you really are."

That's it. Zones and spaces where you can become who you really are.

That's what we're doing now. We're forming a parallel culture. Story by story. Prayer by prayer. Step by step. We are becoming who we really are. More than consumers. Beyond what marketers can imagine.

And as we persevere, a kingdom hope grows. We can transform consumerism. We can resist its pressures on our community life. We can make money flow in new directions and build a more sustainable economy. We can live differently.

This hope is unstoppable. The conspiracy of freedom cannot be silenced. God's future is coming. And so perseverance is always, always worthwhile. As Havel writes:

> This [resistance] went on for years, not without difficulties, but for years. Over time, the truth became stronger and stronger, and at a certain point people began to walk in the streets and to say to the system, "We don't believe you anymore." And the system fell.[15]

▌Detox Diary

This final section is for anyone who wants to take this further.

It contains practical suggestions for the journey – one main action for each chapter, plus a few other ideas too. They've all been road tested and found to lead to simpler, deeper, more generous living.

Now it's up to you.

You can end here.

Or you can start here …

PART ONE: BREAKOUT

Chapter 1: I Am a Consumer

ACTION: What is your consumer story?

A good place to start is to write/consider/discuss with friends what your consumer story is. As David Ford said, "Naming is powerful."[1] Telling our story is part of naming how consumerism works for us.

The following questions might help:

- "My name is _____, and I'm a consumer."
- How did it start?
- What products have I fallen in love with and obsessed over?
- What are the costs of consumerism for me?
- What are the benefits?
- What would greater freedom look like?

▋Chapter 2: I Am Not What I Buy

ACTION: Who am I?

"Who am I?" is the constant refrain of chapter 2. It's worth considering how we think of our identity in consumer terms. For instance:

- Which consumer tribes do I identify with?

- Try dropping a beloved brand or adopting a different tribal consumption pattern. How does it feel? What does it reveal about how tribal branding works?

- What consumer trophies do I own that mark me out as "the best" or "good enough"?

- What would happen if I consumed less? What pressures are at work to keep me in the consumer "arms race"?

▌Chapter 3: I Am Richer Than I Know

ACTION: Thanks

How about spending a week where the only thing you ever do in prayer is say "thank you"? That's nothing but thanksgiving for a full seven-day stretch. Not a single request. Not one.

I was amazed at how helpful this was (so much so that I still do it one day each week—no asking; only thanks).

Other things to consider:

- Try pausing for grace before meals.

- Practice counting up your riches: appreciate the nonfinancial gifts in your life; let your senses engage with the gifts of each day; stay aware of where you come in the rich list of the world's population (check out *www.globalrichlist.com*).

- Make space for the voice of the poor. Ask yourself: Is there a charity I could connect with more? Where are there people local to me who are struggling? What are their names? What are their hopes and aspirations? How can I make space in my life for them?

Chapter 4: We Can Decode the System

ACTION: Decoding

If we can see what the consumer system is doing, it's easier to resist it. Decoding the system has two stages:

First, we can spot where marketing devices are being used. It helps to put what we see into words and discuss it with others. The list of techniques is endless, but we can look for:

- *the deal*–bargains, sales technique and store design
- *the promise*–falsely associating products with desirable values
- *the new*–constant upgrading and new trends
- *the bluff*–a positive, friendly smoke screen
- *the publicity web*–products that lead to more products, and so on
- *the bombardment*–inescapable advertising
- *the threat*–"If you don't buy ..."
- *the double bluff*–outrageous claims that lower our defences

Second, we can undermine the system. This could include:

- unsubscribing from junk mailing lists (e.g., contact the Mail Preference Service–*www.dmachoice.org*; *www.mpsonline.org.uk*).
- decreasing our exposure to desire creators: magazine browsing, web surfing, window-shopping and TV commercials.
- changing the conversation–Are there other things we can talk about than shopping and appearances, or cars and gadgets? (I'm trying not to make gender assumptions as to who talks about what!)
- feeling free to refuse special offers–even freebies!
- calling it what it is (a friend of ours calls DIY programmes "house porn")
- replacing the web of products, brands and advertising images with a deep network of relationships, people and your local environment (see chapter 9).

▌Chapter 5: I Will Not Maximize My Life

ACTION: Limiting

Ask yourself:

- Am I driven or frustrated because I feel life is too short?
- Do I rush through life, cram in activities or break speed limits? If so, why? Do I feel there is not "enough" time?
- How can I enjoy today's gifts simply for what they are?
- Is there any way I could do less but do it better:
  - spending quality time with people?
  - committing to a neighbourhood?
  - prioritizing God's concerns over my ambitions?

PART 2: RHYTHMS OF LIFE

▌Chapter 6: The Power of Stop (Create & Rest)

ACTION: Stop time

OK, don't actually stop time. Plan some "stop time" – time to rest and to be. It could be some moments of peace each morning, or a nightly review of the day. It could be a weekly day of rest (free of work, free of shopping), or a regular retreat. It could be all of these.

Other suggestions that can get us into a rhythm of creation and rest:

- Take an interest in your local environment. Steven Bouma-Prediger asks: "Can you name five trees that live where you do? What flowers bloom where you live? What animals share your place? From what direction do the prevailing winds blow? Where does your water come from? Where does your garbage go?"[2]

- Steward creation: save water and electricity; reduce waste; drive less; eat less meat (excessive meat consumption can be resource intensive, cause carbon emissions and involve inhumane mass-farming methods).

- Be creative: grow stuff; make stuff (wrapping paper, gift cards, presents); make do and mend.

- When buying, ask: Are the goods well made? Were the workers fairly paid? If there were animals involved, how were they treated? Pick one thing you often buy and research the story behind how it is produced.

- Try to do an hour of physical activity each day. It could be anything from a practical hobby to housework to gardening to commuting on foot or by bike. Matthew Sleeth writes, "Many of us have built lives in which we have neither rest nor work. Our jobs do not stress our muscles and joints. Our rest is a series of events in which we give our minds over to machines such as televisions, computers, and DVD players.... Begin to build an hour of work into your daily life. The result will be more life in your day."[3]

- Make Sunday a day to put God at the centre through worship and through enjoying creation.

▌Chapter 7: Life in High-Definition (Presence & Absence)

ACTION: Practice presence

Do you give your full attention to people? For instance, are you reading this while on the phone to a friend? What would it mean for you to be more fully present to others?

Other suggestions for presence and absence:

- Where possible, concentrate on one task at a time and allow for uninterrupted periods during a day. For instance, only accessing email for limited periods in a day can make us more productive, not less.

- Be politely present to neighbours or people on the street with an appropriate greeting (hello, good afternoon, how *you* doin', etc.).

- Put into practice this suggestion from Stephen Cottrell: "Make sure there are a few minutes each day when you are dwelling in complete silence."[4]

- Find what Richard Foster calls "little silences"–tiny gaps of quiet in the day to breathe deeply and reconnect with God.

- Take to heart this excerpt from Dallas Willard, quoting a young Christian who was growing in the discipline of silence for the first time: "The more I practice this discipline, the more I appreciate the strength of silence. The less I become skeptical and judgmental, the more I learn to accept the things I didn't like about others, and the more I learn to accept them as uniquely created in the image of God. The less I talk, the fuller are words spoken at an appropriate time. The more I value others, the more I serve them in small ways, and the more I enjoy and celebrate my life."[5]

Chapter 8: The Art of Waiting (Wait & Enjoy)

ACTION: Pause before you buy

How about this: resist impulse buying. For most purchases, try waiting for a fortnight and see what happens. Ask God to make clear whether or not you really need it. Ask him to bring it to you some other way. Consider carefully: Do I need this? Will it bless others or the environment? Can I make do without?

If two weeks pass and it still feels right to buy, then buy with a clear conscience and enjoy it well!

Other suggestions for waiting and enjoying:

- Try fasting (nothing too dramatic at first) – for thankfulness and to remember the privilege of having food; for prayer and to cultivate a hunger for God; for solidarity with those without food.

- Consider a media fast – from TV, email, or phone (or do the full digital detox and take a break from everything!). What do you miss? What are you more attentive to? What happens to your relationships? What happens to your patterns of work and sleep?

- Take a deep breath and chop up your credit cards. Save and wait for the things you buy.

- Reclaim Advent as a time to prepare for Christmas (rather than an elongated shopfest). We can reclaim Christmas as a time to remember the needy (for instance, by giving simpler presents to each other, then offering what we save as a gift to charity).

- Take time to savour. Enjoy the sensations each day holds. Eat more slowly. Let your senses run wild!

- Throw feasts. Find excuses to celebrate. For the full kingdom banquet experience, don't just invite the usual suspects (Luke 14:12 – 14).

Chapter 9: The Deep Yes (Shallow No & Deep Yes)

ACTION: The list

There's no law against shallow things. We don't turn to plastic if we do too many of them. But thinking carefully about what we do can help us deepen our lives.

Make your own list of what is shallow and deep in your life.

Ask: How can I clear space to invest in deep things?

This list might give you some ideas:

Shallow	→	*Deep*
Buy stuff	→	Make things
Throw away	→	Repair
Send an email	→	Meet for coffee
Fast food	→	Homemade hospitality
DVD	→	Local entertainment
Press Play	→	Learn to play
Presents for kids	→	Presence with kids
Vegging	→	Gardening
Late-night TV	→	Fireside chats
Web surfing	→	Wave surfing
Treadmill	→	Jog
Travel the world	→	Know your neighbours
Headphones	→	Conversation
GPS	→	Ask directions
TV drama	→	Your family
Cheap kids' toys	→	Playing outside
Create a games room	→	Offer a spare room
Glossy website	→	Actual reality
Personality	→	Character
Celebrity	→	Community
Church-shopping	→	Committed fellowship
Bumper-sticker spirituality	→	Wrestling with the Bible

PART 3: ADVENTURES IN GENEROSITY

Chapter 10: Idol

ACTION: Budget

Once a tax collector, always a tax collector. Who else but Zacchaeus would say to Jesus, "I give half of my gross wealth to those with a significantly lower than average income, and I now offer a 400 percent compensation package, subject to a successful complaint"? Some of us might have been tempted to stuff the paperwork and just give the whole lot away!

But at least Zacchaeus had control of his money. He knew how much he had. He was confident that he could calculate and liquidate half of his assets. And, despite his desire to make a grand gesture, he also knew he had an obligation to those he had cheated.

One of the first steps to breaking money's rule is to work out what we have, decide what to do with it, and make sure we're meeting our obligations (including tax – I'm sure Zach would approve!).

So:

- Create a realistic budget of your incoming and outgoing finances for the next year.

- Evaluate the budget: What does it say about your values? Are you living within your means? How does the money you plan to give away compare to the money you plan to save or put in a pension?

- Share your budget with a couple of trusted friends. What do they think? Have they any wise advice?

- Find ways to follow through on your budget (including checking it against receipts or bank statements). Being in control of your finances is a big step to effective generosity.

▌Chapter 11: Openhanded

ACTION: The great sale

Take a deeper step into the flow of giving and receiving. Sell something and give the money to the poor. Something valuable – as valuable as you dare!

NOTE: Buying an immediate replacement for what is sold defeats the object of this action.

Other openhanded suggestions:

- Look again at the examples at the end of the chapter. What challenges or inspires you?

- De-clutter your house and give away what you don't need.

- Adopt a generous lifestyle. How can you fund such a lifestyle? By making thrifty choices (e.g., buy secondhand, take less ambitious vacations)? By earning more? By looking after money better?

- Be vulnerable: Are you willing to live with less financial power and depend on others more? Are you able to receive? Do you ask for what you need? (After all, asking gives someone an opportunity to be blessed through giving!)

- Practice good hospitality (if you're in a position to offer it): Is your hospitality frequent or rare? Is it exhaustingly showy or joyfully simple? Is it exclusive or adventurous?

- Find ways to swap and share locally (e.g., *www.streetbank.com*).

Chapter 12: Tele-vision

ACTION: Connect

The power behind resistance to consumerism is community. We can't do this alone. Who can you join with? Who can you discuss and pray with?

Where can you create signs of restoration and reversal?

Is there a particular cause that God is calling you to?

One last thing.

In April 2009, the Breathe network invited people to make a Promise of Life. It's not a list of rules but a set of aspirations. Perhaps you could make this promise too and share it with others.

The Promise of Life

Because life is a gift, we live thankfully,
Savour what we have,
Pray for what we need.
No longer hurried, distracted, or worried,
We'll walk through each moment with God.

Because everything is a gift, we live with open hands,
Tread lightly on the earth,
Share freely our homes and our things.
No longer restlessly chasing identity,
We'll be known by our love, not our logos.

Because giving is a gift, we live generously,
Give ourselves deeply to family and community,
Give joyfully to those in need.
No longer caught in the consumer dream,
We'll invest in the kingdom of love.

www.breathenetwork.org

▌Acknowledgements

The Consumer Detox Long-Suffering Spouse Award goes to Ailsa Powley. Without your willingness to be eternally embarrassed by these stories, there would be no book.

The Award for Creativity is shared by Phil and Chris. With friends like these, who needs editors?

The Star Contributor Prize goes to everyone involved in the Breathe network. As the stories are told, you'll know who you are …

The Best Supporting Role was played by a wide cast of readers including Gemma Curran, Jon Huntley, Dr Alastair Duke, Perry-May Ward, Liz Russo, Bob Powley, Sam Stephens, Helen Parry, Dr Viv Thomas, Alice Meads and Keir Shreeves.

The Best International Contribution was made by the folks at Zondervan, especially Dudley Delffs, Angela Scheff, Lori VandenBosch, Dirk Buursma and Jennifer Myers.

Finally, the Award for Generosity goes to Simon Downham and the church council of St. Paul's Hammersmith. Thank you for giving me time to write.

▌Notes

▌Chapter 1: I Am a Consumer

1. An important book for me has been Vincent Miller's *Consuming Religion* (New York: Continuum, 2004).

   How can we define consumerism? The consuming of goods is as old as the hills. But consumerism is more than this. David Lyon defines it as "a particular focusing of social and personal life on the processes of consuming" ("Consumerism," in *New Dictionary of Christian Ethics and Pastoral Theology* [Downers Grove, Ill.: InterVarsity, 1995], 256). Most commentators trace it back to the period after World War II, which is when the term *consumerism* was coined.

   Consumerism is not the same as capitalism (so if you're wondering if it has gone too far, that doesn't make you a Communist!). In fact, what we currently have is more than just consumer capitalism. Consuming is so vital to our identity and our society that we almost need a new word for it. Neal Lawson suggests *turbo-consumerism* (see *All Consuming* [London: Penguin, 2009]).

2. David Ford, *The Shape of Living* (Grand Rapids: Baker, 1997), 19.

3. Andrew Fischer of Omaha, Nebraska, put his forehead for sale on eBay and received $37,375 to advertise a snoring remedy for one month.

   In 2006, the BBC reported that in some Iranian town squares, young men and women were seen advertising their own kidneys. One of their signs read: "Immediate offer! Kidney for sale, young man, 22, healthy, blood type O positive. Tel 09122 …"

4. At last count it was at least two for Europe and nearly five for America (see Hilary Osborne, "Humans Using Resources of Two Planets, WWF Warns," October 24, 2006, *http://www.guardian.co.uk/environment/2006/oct/24/conservation.internationalnews*). See *www.ecofoot.org* to calculate your own global footprint.

5. Miller, *Consuming Religion*, 16.

   Naomi Klein (*No Logo* [London: Flamingo, 2000], esp. chap. 9), among many others, has exposed the conditions in the "outsourced" factories of some of our major global brands.

6. Old Testament scholar Walter Brueggemann (*Theology of the Old Testament* [Philadelphia: Fortress, 1997], 718) pulls no punches: "The dominant metanarrative of Western society … is military consumerism.… This metanarrative has, as its 'consumer' component, the conviction that well-being, security, and happiness are the result of getting, having, using, and consuming, activities that may be done without restraint or limit, even at the expense of others. This construal of reality has its 'military' component in the conviction that having a disproportion of whatever it takes to enjoy well-being, security, and happiness is appropriate, and that the use of force, coercion, or violence, either to secure or to maintain a disproportion, is completely congruent with this notion of happiness."

7. Oliver James, "On the Money," *The Observer,* January 1, 2006, *www.guardian.co .uk/lifeandstyle/2006/jan/01/healthandwellbeing.features.* As philosopher Ivan Illich said, "In a consumer society there are inevitably two kinds of slaves: the prisoners of addiction and the prisoners of envy."

8. Ben Okri, "Our False Oracles Have Failed," *The Times,* October 30, 2008, *www.times online.co.uk/tol/comment/columnists/guest_contributors/article5041585.ece.*

9. For instance, according to James Morris, executive director of the United Nations World Food Programme, China has "lifted 300 million of its own people out of poverty in less than a generation – surely one of the greatest achievements of the 20th century" (speaking in Beijing, December 2004).

10. Cited in Worldwatch Institute, "State of the World 2004: Consumption by the Numbers" (January 8, 2004), *http://www.worldwatch.org/node/1783.*

11. As economist Herman Daly pointed out, there is such a thing as "uneconomic growth," where the numbers go up but life doesn't get any better. However, there are ways to invest in the economy that make society more healthy, not less:

   - We can invest in ethical banking or in microfinance loans to businesses in developing countries.
   - We can create "green collar" jobs in increasing efficiency, developing recycling and harnessing renewable energy.
   - We can buy Fair Trade (so that overseas producers can plan for a future based on stable prices and use any profits to invest locally).
   - We can buy less, but buy products made to last. Better stuff is often more expensive (so it creates plenty of economic activity), but if it lasts longer, it leads to less waste.
   - We can give to charity and buy gifts for friends (or strangers!).

   All of this pumps money into the global economy. All of it creates wealth; it just creates it differently. A similar amount of money is involved; we're just making it flow in new directions. In other words, if the economy is a car, it does need fuel, but there's more than one way to power an engine! Some great thinking in this area is being done by The New Economics Foundation. Check out *www.new economics.org* or *The New Economics* by David Boyle and Andrew Simms (London: Earthscan, 2009).

12. Ford, *Shape of Living*, 19.

13. Clive Hamilton, *Overconsumption in Britain* (Canberra: The Australia Institute, 2003), *www.tai.org.au/documents/dp_fulltext/DP57.pdf.*

14. Chuck Palahniuk, *Fight Club* (New York: Vintage, 1997), 149.

15. Numbers 11:4–5.

▌Chapter 2: I Am Not What I Buy

1. Vincent Miller (*Consuming Religion* [New York: Continuum, 2003], 115–16) writes: "As previous markers of social identity such as class and ethnicity … changed, individuals were increasingly dependent on factors such as appearance and 'personality' to prosper socially.… People spend money on personal-appearance products and services, clothing, and luxury items such as watches and cars, not simply out of desire for those particular products, or even because they enjoy reimagining and recreating themselves, but to maintain their status in society.… Keeping up with the Joneses has become a full-time job."

2. Quoted in Joseph Heath and Andrew Potter, *The Rebel Sell* (Oxford: Capstone, 2006), 217.

3. The arms race analogy comes from Joseph Heath and Andrew Potter (*The Rebel Sell*, 117). Sociologist Zygmunt Bauman (*Consuming Life* [Cambridge: Polity, 2007], 111) points out that the real commodity in this process isn't what we buy; it's *us*. We're the ones who are constantly rebranding ourselves. We're the ones trying to convince the world that we have what it takes, that there's a niche for us, that we are worth investing in. "Consumers are driven by the need to 'commoditize' themselves—make themselves into attractive commodities.… They must accurately watch the vacillations of what is demanded … and follow the market trends: an unenviable, often utterly exhausting task, given the notorious volatility of consumer markets."

4. Don Slater, *Consumer Culture and Modernity* (Cambridge: Polity, 1997), 10.

5. Radiohead, "Fake Plastic Trees," by Yorke/O'Brien/Greenwood/Greenwood/ Selway © 1994 Warner/Chappell Music Ltd. (PRS). All rights reserved. Used by permission.

6. Chuck Palahniuk, *Fight Club* (New York: Vintage, 1997), 143.

7. Palahniuk, *Fight Club*, 169.

8. Matthew 5:44, 46–47; 6:31–32.

9. Simon Walker, *Leading Out of Who You Are* (Carlisle: Piquant, 2007), 105–6, with slight changes. Walker suggests that only God can play this role. He continues, "This Other has to be divine–but they also have to be personal. A force or way of being or organising principle in the world is no good to me: I can't be loved and accepted and approved of by a cosmic energy.... If I can find such a relationship, it will begin to make courageous, self-sacrificial living possible."

▌Chapter 3: I Am Richer Than I Know

1. Thorstein Veblen, "Why Is Economics Not an Evolutionary Science," *The Quarterly Journal of Economics* 12 (1898): 373.

2. See Charles F. Kettering, "Keep the Consumer Dissatisfied," *Nation's Business* 17 (January 1929): 30–31, 79.

3. Clive Hamilton, *Downshifting in Britain: A Sea-Change in the Pursuit of Happiness* (The Australia Institute, 2003), *https://www.tai.org.au/index.php?q=node%2F19& pubid=58&act=display*.

4. Thorsten Moritz, "New Testament Voices for an Addicted Society," in *Christ and Consumerism*, Craig Bartholomew and Thorsten Moritz, eds. (Carlisle: Paternoster, 2000), 76.

5. Some people argue about whether the universe "proves" God or not. I think this misses the point. The universe isn't an argument; it's a gift. Insisting on irrefutable evidence that God created the universe is like taking a birthday present back to the shop and demanding to see proof of purchase. As the philosopher Albert Borgmann says, "Creation is donation not causation." *Power Failure* (Grand Rapids: Brazos, 2003), 73.

6. Thomas Traherne, *Centuries of Meditations* (1908; repr.; New York: Cosimo, 2007), 17, 19–20.

7. See Gillian Butler and Tony Hope, *Manage Your Mind* (Oxford: Oxford University Press, 1995), 177–78. The original story is told by Philip Wakeham ("Living Target," in *Seamen and the Sea*, R. Hope, ed. [London: George Harrap & Co., 1965]).

8. Cited in J. John and Mark Stibbe, *Box of Delights* (Oxford: Monarch, 2001), 151.

9. The study *Happiness and Economics* by Bruno S. Fey and Alois Stutzer (Princeton, N.J.: Princeton University Press, 2002) found that once a country's Gross Domestic Product (GDP) reached around $8,000 per head, economic growth was no longer matched by increases in average happiness. According to one report, Britain's growth in national happiness peaked in 1975, the year I was born (could there be a link?!).

10. Interview with Alice Thomson, *The Daily Telegraph*, April 2006. Historian Meic Pearse expands on this theme: "Since we have been superrich for several generations now, we have come to take prosperity for granted. For us, death at a young age – or even any time before our late sixties or so – seems to be an abnormal tragedy. If a relative dies young, we do not merely grieve; our lives are devastated. We question the existence of God.... Though we entertain ourselves with a constant stream of simulated violence on TV, if we witness a real killing, or a battle, we are far more prone than traditional people to suffer mental or emotional breakdown. We are less resilient than our forebears. [And] since no one will now starve if my family breaks up, a major bond that has held all families together has been removed" ("Growing Up Is Hard to Do," *EG* magazine [London Institute for Contemporary Christianity, October 2008]. Used by permission).

11. The duke, in William Shakespeare, *Measure for Measure*, 2nd ed. (London: Taylor and Francis, 1965), 68 (Act 3, Scene 1).

12. Quoted in Tom Sine, *Mustard Seed versus McWorld* (Oxford: Monarch, 1999), 111.

13. Barry Schwartz, *The Paradox of Choice: Why More Is Less* (New York: HarperCollins, 2004). At Schwartz's local hi-fi store, the different products available enabled over 6,500,000 possible music player configurations. Could this be too much choice?

14. Rhidian Brook's "Thought for the Day," broadcast on BBC Radio 4, February 2, 2006. Used by permission.

❚ Chapter 4: We Can Decode the System

1. The U.S. figure is estimated at $412 billion by Outsell, Inc. (press release, July 14, 2008, *www.outsellinc.com*); the figure for Western Europe, $125 billion, comes from Martin Olausson's "Western Europe Advertising Forecast 2006–2013" (*www.strategyanalytics.com*).

2. At the last count, Shell was bigger than Venezuela; IBM was bigger than Singapore; and Sony was bigger than Pakistan. See Sarah Anderson and John Cavanagh, *Top 200: The Rise of Corporate Global Power* (Washington, D.C.: Institute for Policy Studies, 2000).

3. Paco Underhill, *Why We Buy: The Science of Shopping*, 2nd ed. (New York: Simon & Schuster, 2009), 29. To his credit, Underhill reports one of the worst examples of consumer hype, courtesy of a national U.S. clothing store. Their vice president of merchandising once boasted about a set of young women's T-shirts: "We buy them in Sri Lanka for three dollars each.... Then we bring them over here and sew in washing instructions in French and English ... notice we don't say the shirts are made in France. But you can infer that if you like. Then we merchandise ... them—we fold them just right on a tasteful tabletop display, and on the wall behind it we hang a huge, gorgeous photograph of a beautiful woman in an exotic locale wearing the shirt. We shoot it so it looks like a million bucks. Then we call it an Expedition T-shirt, and we sell it for thirty-seven dollars. And we sell a lot of them too" (p. 220).

4. Germaine Greer, *The Female Eunuch* (New York: McGraw-Hill, 1980), 51–52.

5. William T. Cavanaugh, *Being Consumed* (Grand Rapids: Eerdmans, 2008), 47.

6. Matthew Sleeth gives a great example of the technological bluff: "What happens when we stop using a manual lawn mower? The nonmotorized variety is inexpensive and quiet and uses no fossil fuels. The push mower requires us to exert energy; thus, we obtain exercise and become healthier. By its very nature, the manual mower dictates a reasonably sized lawn. What happens when we decide to save labor and purchase a gas-powered lawn mower? It spews out poisonous fumes, which we inhale. The mower is loud and damages our hearing; mowing our lawn requires little effort, and our muscles atrophy.... Finally, when we gain too much weight, we drive a two-ton vehicle to a health club where we can pay to work against the resistance of a machine. Why not just back up and push our own mower?" *Serve God, Save the Planet* (Grand Rapids: Zondervan, 2006), 91–92.

7. About Lovemarks: "How Do I Know a Lovemark?" *www.lovemarks.com*.

8. Steve Connor, "Official: Coke takes over parts of the brain that Pepsi can't reach," *The Independent*, October 17, 2004. Of course, if you can establish brand loyalty with little children (I don't know, like with some kind of Meal that makes them Happy), the subconscious bond to the company will be so much stronger.

9. Brian Walsh and Sylvia Keesmaat, *Colossians Remixed* (Downers Grove, Ill.: InterVarsity, 2004), 63. This book contains some explosive reflections on the consumer empire.

10. Mark A. Burch, *Stepping Lightly* (Gabriola Island, BC: New Society Publishers, 2000).

11. Vincent Miller, *Consuming Religion* (New York: Continuum, 2003), 125.

12. Media research company Nielson counted 4,636 occurrences of product placement during season seven of *American Idol*, many of which featured Coca-Cola.

13. Zygmunt Bauman, *Consuming Life* (Cambridge: Polity, 2007), 99.

14. Revelation 13:16–17.

15. Excerpt from *The Matrix* copyright © Warner Bros. Inc. All rights reserved. Used with permission of Warner Bros. Inc. and the Wachowski Brothers. Fans of *The Matrix* will know that Neo eventually brings peace to the world not by ruthlessly crushing his enemies but by offering himself to achieve reconciliation. For what it's worth, this is a better model for dealing with consumerism than a kind of Star Wars campaign to "destroy the evil empire."

The Christian claim is that Jesus has enabled peace by shedding his own blood (not that of his enemies), and so now all things can assume their proper place in the universe (see Colossians 1:16, 19–20; 2:14–15). In the same way, our aim shouldn't be the destruction of the global economy. Our aim should be that business and advertising assume their proper place: that they serve human flourishing, and are kept accountable to the principles of transparency, fairness and compassion.

16. This is where history gets messy. Did Constantine (the first Christian emperor) co-opt Christianity to his ambitions? Did Christianity later sell out to imperial power? To an extent, yes. But we do know that the early church, at great cost, retained a counterimperial voice. In a sense the church neither got swallowed up by empire nor triumphed over it. It transformed empire. For instance, before the advent of Christianity, it was routine Roman practice to leave unwanted babies outdoors to die. The church made a difference, and it safeguarded the

message that ever since has challenged unjust power (like when Polish Catholicism contributed to the fall of Communism or when the united action of some South African Christians helped to overturn apartheid).

17. In this, they took a cue from their founder, who, instead of rebelling over Roman taxes quipped, "If you want the money badly enough to stamp your face on it, you can keep it!" (or words to that effect). He also stood before the might of the Roman Empire, with his life in the balance, and said, "All this power isn't really yours" (again, a free translation). No wonder his followers saw through empire.

18. Rodney Stark, *Cities of God* (New York: HarperCollins, 2006), 30.

Chapter 5: I Will Not Maximize My Life

1. N. H. Kleinbaum, *Dead Poets Society* (New York: Hyperion, 1989), 26–27, a novelization of the motion picture written by Tom Schulman.

2. Kleinbaum, *Dead Poets Society*, 25–26.

3. American psychologist Thomas Pyszcynski has argued that the pursuit of shopping has become "a protective shield designed to control the potential for terror that results from awareness of the horrifying possibility that we humans are merely transient animals groping to survive in a meaningless universe, destined only to die and decay" (quoted in John Naish, *Enough* [London: Hodder, 2009], 86).

4. Richard Layard and Judy Dunn, *A Good Childhood: Searching for Values in a Competitive Age* (London: Penguin, 2009), 6.

5. For what it's worth, there are several reasons not to confuse "life to the full" with the consumer dream.

When Jesus speaks of life, he is speaking above all about knowing God. We know this because he tells us: "Now this is eternal life: that they know you, the only true God" (John 17:3). It's not about a level of lifestyle, but a quality of relationship with the Father. In fact, Jesus explicitly warned that "life does not consist in an abundance [same basic word: *perisseuô*] of possessions" (Luke 12:15).

So why is it life "to the full" or "abundantly"? Because even death can't stop it (at a time when not all God's people believed in resurrection, this was no small claim). "Life" is to know God; "to the full" is to know God forever. The abundance is mainly an abundance of time. Throughout John's gospel this is the pattern. The spring of water Jesus brings quenches thirst now and "wells up to eternal life" (John 4:14). The bread he offers feeds us now and also "endures" (John 6:27). The one who believes in him will "live" and "never die" (John 11:25–26). In each case Jesus offers life now and life later. John 10 is no different. Jesus talks of a thief who kills and destroys (John 10:10; see 10:28). All other offers of life cannot last. Only Jesus can make the "sheep" truly safe. Only he came to give us life—now and always.

6. See Mark 12:44 for the leftover money; Luke 15:17 for the spare food; Matthew 14:20 for the crumbs (in these cases, the verb form *perisseuô* is used).

7. See Romans 5:15; 2 Corinthians 8:1–3: "Brothers and sisters, we want you to know about the grace that God has given the Macedonian churches. In the midst of a very severe trial, their *overflowing* joy and their extreme poverty *welled up* [overflowed] in rich generosity. For I testify that they gave as much as they were able, and even beyond their ability."

8. H. A. Williams, *The Joy of God* (London: Continuum, 1979), 16.

9. Acts 17:25.

10. Lamentations 3:22–23. "What has really happened during the last seven days and nights? Seven times we have been dissolved into darkness as we shall be dissolved into dust; our very selves, as far as we know, have been wiped out of the world of living things; and seven times we have been raised alive like Lazarus, and found all our limbs and senses unaltered, with the coming of the day." G. K. Chesterton, quoted in Eugene Peterson, *Christ Plays in Ten Thousand Places* (Grand Rapids: Eerdmans, 2005), 119.

11. Romans 13:11–12. Sit back, relax and enjoy this incredible quote on triple enjoyment from Miroslav Volf (*Free of Charge* [Grand Rapids: Zondervan, 2005], 110): "A rich self has a distinct attitude toward the past, the present, and the future. It surveys the past with *gratitude* for what it has received, not with any annoyance about what it hasn't achieved or about how little it has been given. A rich self lives in the present with *contentment*. Rather than never having enough of anything except for the burdens others place on it, it is 'always having enough of everything' (2 Corinthians 9:8 [NRSV]). It still strives, but it strives out of a satisfied fullness, not out of the emptiness of craving. A rich self looks to the future with *trust*. It gives rather than holding back in fear of coming out too short, because it believes God's promise that God will take care of it. Finite and endangered, a rich self still gives, because its life is 'hidden in Christ' in the infinite, unassailable, and utterly generous God, the Lord of the present, the past, and the future (see Colossians 3:3)."

12. Matthew 11:27–29 MSG.

13. Philip James Bailey, "We Live in Deeds," from *Festus* (quoted in *Masterpieces of Religious Verse*, ed. James Dalton Morrison [Grand Rapids: Baker, 1977], 358).

Chapter 6: The Power of Stop

1. Marcia K. Hornok, "Psalm 23, Antithesis," first published in *Discipleship Journal* 60 (November-December 1990). Used by permission.

2. Genesis 1:31–2:3.

3. "So God created human beings in his own image.... God blessed them and said to them, 'Be fruitful and increase in number; fill the earth and subdue it' " (Genesis 1:27–28).

4. Sabbath was a check on rapacious trading (Jeremiah 17:19–27; Amos 8:5); it was a curb on slavery for a people who had once been slaves (Deuteronomy 5:12–15). It even extended to cancelling debts and resting the land every seven years (Nehemiah 10:31).

5. 2 Chronicles 36:17–21 NIV.

6. Norman Wirzba, *Living The Sabbath: Discovering the Rhythms of Rest and Delight* (Grand Rapids: Brazos, 2006), 38.

7. Revelation 1:16 says of Jesus, "His face was like the sun shining in all its brilliance." Psalm 121:3 puts it like this: "He who watches over you will not slumber; indeed, he who watches over Israel will neither slumber nor sleep."

8. G. K. Chesterton, *What's Wrong with the World* (New York.: Dodd, Mead and Company, 1910), 169.

9. Do they write songs like this anymore?

   "O sabbath rest by Galilee! / O calm of hills above! / Where Jesus knelt to share with Thee / The silence of eternity, / Interpreted by love" (John Greenleaf Whittier, "Dear Lord and Father of Mankind," 1872).

▌Chapter 7: Life in High-Definition

1. Gerard Manley Hopkins, *God's Grandeur* (1877; repr., New York: Dover, 1995), 15.

   The world is charged with the grandeur of God.
   It will flame out, like shining from shook foil;
   It gathers to a greatness, like the ooze of oil
   Crushed.

2. Linda Stone, summary description of her "Keynote Address: 'Attention: The *Real* Aphrodisiac,'" O'Reilly Emerging Technology Conference, March 6–9, 2006, *http://conferences.oreillynet.com/cs/et2006/view/e–sess/8290.*

3. Linda Stone, "Thoughts on Continuous Partial Attention." Used by permission: *www.lindastone.net.* Quotation from *Neue Gegenwart* magazine, *www.neuegegen wart.de/ausgabe51/continuouspartialattention.htm.*

4. 1 John 1:1 NLT.

5. "Jesus often withdrew to lonely places and prayed" (Luke 5:16).

6. Dietrich Bonhoeffer, *Life Together* (New York: Harper, 1954), 77.

7. Williams' words were inspired by Desmond Tutu's ability to delight in being who God made him to be. Quoted by permission of the Archbishop of Canterbury from his short essay, "Tutu enjoying Tutu," in *Tutu As I Know Him: On a Personal Note,* ed. Lavinia Crawford-Browne (Roggebaai, South Africa: Umizi), 161.

8. Mark 1:11 NRSV.

9. The parable is found in Luke 15:11–32. Middle Eastern scholar Kenneth E. Bailey (*The Cross and the Prodigal*, 2nd ed. [Downers Grove: InterVarsity, 2005], 67) writes: "In the Middle East a man of [the father's] age and position *always* walks in a slow, dignified fashion.... But now the father *races* down the road. To do so, he must take the front edge of his robes in his hand like a teenager. When he does this, his legs show in what is considered a humiliating posture. All of this is painfully shameful for him. The loiterers in the street will be distracted from tormenting the prodigal and will instead run after the father, amazed at seeing this respected village elder shaming himself publicly. It is his 'compassion' that leads the father to race out to his son. He knows what his son will face in the village. He takes upon himself the shame and humiliation due the prodigal."

10. Mother Teresa, *The Love of Christ* (New York: Harper, 1992), 8–9.

11. William P. Young, *The Shack* (Newbury Park, Calif.: Windblown Media), 108–13.

12. William Barclay, *The Gospel of John: Volume 1* (Daily Study Bible; Philadelphia: Westminster, 1955), 225–26.

▌Chapter 8: The Art of Waiting

1. Eugene Peterson, *Under the Unpredictable Plant* (Grand Rapids: Eerdmans, 1992), 96.

2. Ian Stackhouse makes this observation about Monet's water lily paintings in his book *The Day Is Yours* (Carlisle, UK: Paternoster, 2008).

3. M. Scott Peck, *The Road Less Traveled* (New York: Simon & Schuster, 1978), 18.

4. Wendy Mogel, *The Blessing of a Skinned Knee* (New York: Simon & Schuster, 2001), 32, 130.

5. 2 Peter 3:9 MSG.

6. Rick Warren, *The Purpose Driven Life* (Grand Rapids: Zondervan, 2002), 202.

7. Richard Foster, *Freedom of Simplicity* (New York: Harper, 1981), 122.

8. Song of Songs 8:6–7.

9. Paul writes of our and God's groaning in Romans 8:22–26; Jesus' beatitudes ("Blessed are those who mourn") are found in Matthew 5.

10. John Smith, *Cutting Edge* (Oxford: Monarch, 1992), 28–29.

11. Luke 13:29.

12. Fyodor Dostoyevsky, *The Idiot*, trans. David Magarshack (London: Penguin, 1955), 57–58. In December 1849, twenty years before he wrote this passage, Dostoyevsky himself was pardoned at the last minute from what turned out to be a mock execution. Immediately afterward, he wrote to his brother, "Life is a gift. Life is happiness. Every minute will be an eternity of happiness" (quoted in Joseph Frank, *Dostoevsky: The Years of Ordeal* [Princeton, N.J.: Princeton University Press, 1990], 62).

13. Mike Yaconelli, *Dangerous Wonder* (Colorado Springs: NavPress, 1998), 87.

14. "The present moment holds infinite riches beyond your wildest dreams.... The will of God is manifest in each moment, an immense ocean which the heart only fathoms insofar as it overflows with faith, trust, and love." Jean-Pierre De Caussade, eighteenth-century spiritual writer, in *The Sacrament of the Present Moment* (New York: Harper, 1982), 62.

▌Chapter 9: The Deep Yes

1. A brilliant take on shallow/deep is the film *Wall-E* (Disney/Pixar, 2008). Or consider this from Albert Borgmann: "The great defensive devices that protect us from hunger, cold, disease, darkness, confinement, and exertion have been in place for at least a generation now.... Technology now mimics the great breakthroughs of the past, assuring us that it is an imposition to have to open a garage door, walk behind a lawn mower, or wait twenty minutes for a frozen dinner to be ready. Being given riding lawn mowers, garage door openers, and microwave ovens, we feel for a moment the power of wielding the magic wand. The remembrance of strain and impatience, of relative powerlessness, yields to a sentiment of ease and competence. We seem to move with the effortlessness of youth, with the vigor of an athlete, with the quickness of the great chef. But it is an entirely parasitic feeling that feeds off the disappearance of toil; it is not animated by the full-bodied exercise of skill, gained through discipline and renewed through intimate commerce with the world. On the contrary, our contact with reality has been attenuated to the pushing of buttons and the turning of handles. The results are guaranteed by a machinery that is not of our design and often beyond our understanding. Hence the feelings of liberation quickly fade; the new devices lose their glamour and meld into the inconspicuous periphery of normalcy; boredom replaces exhilaration" (*Technology and the Character of Contemporary Life* [Chicago: University of Chicago Press, 1984], 140).

2. Sarfraz Manzoor, "The Spices of Life," *The Guardian*, January 1, 2008.

3. Quoted in Ben Fenton, "Junk Culture Is Poisoning Our Children," *Daily Telegraph*, September 12, 2006.

4. Recent British stats suggest that children aged eleven to fifteen spend an average of fifty-three hours a week in front of a computer or TV screen; that's 55 percent of their waking lives (*The Week*, September 24, 2005); 80 percent of five- to sixteen-year-olds have their own TV (*ChildWise Trends*, 2009), 63 percent of children watch TV before going to bed, and 58 percent with the evening meal (*ChildWise/The Guardian*, 2006).

5. The American Academy of Pediatrics recommends that children under two years old avoid all TV and electronic media (see *www.screentime.org*).

6. Letter to *The Daily Telegraph*, "Modern Life Leads to More Depression Among Children," *Daily Telegraph*, September 12, 2006.

7. Bill Bailey, "Bill Bailey's Remarkable Guide to the Orchestra." Used by permission. Novelist Marcel Proust wrote, in one of his typically long sentences, of "that abominable and sensual act called *reading the newspaper*, thanks to which all the misfortunes and cataclysms in the universe over the past twenty-four hours, the battles which cost the lives of fifty thousand men, the murders, the strikes, the bankruptcies, the fires, the poisonings, the suicides, the divorces, the cruel emotions of statesmen and actors, are transformed for us, who don't even care, into a morning treat, blending in wonderfully, in a particularly exciting and tonic way, with the recommended ingestion of a few sips of *Café au lait*" (quoted in Alain de Botton, *Proust Can Change Your Life* [London: Picador, 1997], 37).

8. Vincent Miller, *Consuming Religion* (New York: Continuum, 2004), 133–34. Are we close here to what J. G. Ballard had in mind when he began his novel *Kingdom Come*? "The suburbs dream of violence. Asleep in their drowsy villas, sheltered by benevolent shopping malls, they wait passionately for the nightmares that will wake them into a more passionate world" (London: Fourth Estate, 2006), 3.

9. This compares with volunteers who spent thirty minutes reading about the same events. Research by Dr Attila Szabo (published in *The International Journal of Behavioral Medicine*, 2005).

10. Miller McPherson, Lynn Smith-Lovin and Matthew E. Brashears, "Social Isolation in America," *American Sociological Review* 71 (2006): 353–75.

11. Rowan Williams, *The Truce of God* (London: Fount, 1983), 97.

12. Stephen Covey, "Work-Life Balance: A Different Cut" (*www.Forbes.com*, March 2007). Reprinted by permission of Forbes Media LLC © 2010.

▌Chapter 10: Idol

1. Colossians 3:5.

2. Tim Keller, "Treasure vs. Money," sermon preached at Redeemer Church, New York (*www.redeemer.com*), May 22, 1999. Used by permission.

3. *Do not eat the food of a stingy man,*
     do not crave his delicacies;
   for he is the kind of man
     who is always thinking about the cost.
   "Eat and drink," he says to you,
     but his heart is not with you.
   You will vomit up the little you have eaten
     and will have wasted your compliments.
   Proverbs 23:6–8 NIV

4. The parable of the prodigal son in Luke 15:11–32 illustrates this double tension perfectly (which is why Luke explains that Jesus told it to "Pharisees" who were angry about "sinners," 15:1–2). The younger son indulges in a life of extravagant compromise, but the father welcomes him home. The elder son (whose story, though less famous, occupies just as much space) is filled with indignation, but again the father goes out to him and appeals for him to return. The story is a defence of Jesus' ministry: through him the Father is holding out his hands to both conspicuous sinners on the one hand and the smouldering self-righteous on the other.

5. Luke 12:15, 22, 29–34.

6. The parable of the workers in the vineyard (Matthew 20:1–16):

   1 day's work = 1 denarius; ½ day's work = 1 denarius; 1 hour's work = 1 denarius

   The parable of the rich farmer (Luke 12:13–21):

   1 small barn's capacity + a bigger barn's extra capacity = 0

   The widow's gift (Luke 21:1–4):

   2 small copper coins } (is more than) the huge offerings of the rich

   As Jonathan Lamb (*Integrity* [Nottingham, UK: Inter-Varsity, 2006], 166) puts it, "Jesus … crept into life's window and swapped the price tags round."

7. See Luke 6:30, 34–35: "Give to everyone who asks you, and if anyone takes what belongs to you, do not demand it back…. And if you lend to those from whom you expect repayment, what credit is that to you? Even sinners lend to sinners, expecting to be repaid in full. But love your enemies, do good to them, and lend to them without expecting to get anything back."

8. The child's food (John 6:7–9); tax from a fish (Matthew 17:24–27): "The collectors of the two-drachma temple tax came to Peter and asked, 'Doesn't your teacher pay the temple tax?' … Jesus said to him … 'go to the lake and throw out your line.

'sh you catch; open its mouth and you will find a four-drachma coin.
it to them for my tax and yours.' "

, is told in Mark 14:3–9. Even a passion for justice can become obsessive.
Jacques Ellul (*False Presence of the Kingdom* [New York: Seabury, 1972], 70–71)
comments helpfully: "It is enough to bear [the suffering] of one's neighbour. Once
again, we encounter the very bad presumption of putting ourselves in the place of
Jesus Christ....

"That does not mean that we are to be indifferent to the sufferings of mankind!
But it does mean that my only actual concern is the one which is near enough
to me, and close enough to my size, so that I might *really* do something about
it. Revelation, in its rigorous realism, does not ask us to torture ourselves
over universal ideas and information, nor to lose sleep over news items from
everywhere."

10. The Bible has no problem with what is sometimes called the creation of wealth.
It is more concerned with who gets the proceeds and also with the dangers of
holding on to wealth at others' expense. Augustine in his *Commentary on Psalm
147* put it like this: "When superfluous things are possessed, others' property is
possessed."

11. Matthew 7:21; Mark 12:28–34.

12. Tom Sine, *Mustard Seed versus McWorld* (Grand Rapids: Baker, 1999), 155. Vincent
Miller (*Consuming Religion* [New York: Continuum, 2004], 88, 142) suggests that
popular Western Christianity is superficial ("abstracted sentiment divorced from
practice") precisely because anything more radical would challenge our consumer
patterns too much. Once we've slotted our lives into the groove of single-family
homes, driven workplaces and high-consumption leisure time, can Christianity ever be any more than a hobby? What if, instead of allowing Christianity to
redefine consumerism, we've allowed consumerism to domesticate Christianity?
In which case, where does our deepest allegiance lie? Provocative stuff.

13. Ron Sider, *The Scandal of the Evangelical Conscience: Why Are Christians Living
Just Like the Rest of the World?* (Grand Rapids: Baker, 2005), 117.

14. Tim Keller (*The Reason for God* [New York: Dutton, 2008], 276) observes: "If you
center your life and identity on a 'noble cause,' you will divide the world into 'good'
and 'bad' and demonize your opponents. Ironically, you will be controlled by your
enemies. Without them, you have no purpose." Keller argues that only belief in
God can give us both the inspiration we need to change and yet also a humility
that can save us from being judgmental (see Keller's chapter 10).

15. Mark 1:15.

16. Richard Foster, *Money, Sex and Power* (London: Hodder, 1985), 60–61.

▎Chapter 11: Openhanded

1. Deuteronomy 15:7–8 (Jesus picks up this language in Matthew 5:42).

2. James 1:17. James knows he has to tackle issues of favouritism, injustice and lack of compassion. But he kicks off by getting the right foundation in place: God "gives generously to all without finding fault" (James 1:5).

3. Quoted by Dallas Willard, who explains this brilliantly in *The Divine Conspiracy* (London: Fount, 1998), 72.

4. Hebrews 6:5.

5. The full gift list: forgiveness (Matthew 18:21–35); royal status (Romans 8:17, "co-heirs with Christ"); one hundred times what we give up (Mark 10:29–30); all things (1 Corinthians 3:21–23).

6. "The Great Salmon Run," *Nature's Great Events* (wildlife documentary series), BBC television, 2009.

7. Timothy Keller, *The Reason for God* (New York: Dutton, 2008), 216–17 (in fact, the whole of chapter 14 is amazing).

8. 1 John 4:16; Jeremiah 22:16.

9. Eugene Peterson, *Run with the Horses*, 2nd ed. (Downers Grove, Ill.: InterVarsity, 1983), 44–45.

10. "Jesus himself said: 'It is more blessed to give than to receive'" (Acts 20:35); Paul wrote, "Excel in this grace of giving" (2 Corinthians 8:7).

11. Edward Arlington Robinson, "Captain Craig," in *Collected Poems* (New York: Macmillan, 1922), 115.

12. Mike Riddell, *Godzone* (Oxford: Lion, 1992), 40.

13. Quoted in Miroslav Volf, *Free of Charge* (Grand Rapids: Zondervan, 2005), 50. For what it's worth, the apostle Paul taught this too. We can receive all things with joy, "overflowing with thankfulness" (Colossians 2:7). But we don't have to seek

anything more than life's basics: "if we have food and clothing, we will be content with that" (1 Timothy 6:8). Being so thankful and content, it should be no problem for us to give. Besides, whatever we pass on to others, God is able to repay "so that [we] can be generous on every occasion" (2 Corinthians 9:11). It's almost too easy – apart from the entire weight of human selfishness. Like I say, apart from that, it's easy!

14. Theologian Jürgen Moltmann (*The Open Church: Invitation to a Messianic Lifestyle* [London: SCM Press, 1978]) comments: "A closed human being no longer has any hope. Such a person is full of anxiety. A closed society no longer has any future. It kills the hope for life of those who stand on its periphery, and then it finally destroys itself. Hope is lived, and it comes alive when we go outside of ourselves and, in joy and pain, take part in the life of others."

15. Quoted in Coretta Scott King, *The Words of Martin Luther King, Jr.* (New York: Newmarket, 1983), 17.

16. Philippians 2:6–7; 2 Corinthians 8:9; John 13:3–5.

17. C. S. Lewis, *The Problem of Pain* (New York: Macmillan, 1961), 140. Lewis continues: "From the highest to the lowest, self exists to be abdicated and, by that abdication, becomes the more truly self, to be thereupon yet the more abdicated, and so forever. This is not a … law which we can escape…. What is outside the system of self-giving is … simply and solely Hell…. That fierce imprisonment of the self is but the obverse of the self-giving which is absolute reality."

18. Luke 14:25–33.

19. 2 Corinthians 8:7–9.

20. 1 John 3:16–18.

21. Richard Foster, *Freedom of Simplicity* 2nd ed. (London: Hodder, 2005), 113, 117.

22. Acts 4:32–35.

23. "The Apology of Aristides the Philosopher" (written ca. AD 125), in *Ante-Nicene Fathers* (1887; repr., Peabody, Mass.: Hendrickson, 1995), 9:277.

24. Lucian of Samosata, "The Passing of Peregrinus," in *Lucian: Vol. 7* (Loeb Classical Library).

25. Prophet and activist Shane Claiborne (who has more right than most to get legalistic about all this) rightly comments (*Irresistible Revolution* [Grand Rapids:

Zondervan, 2006], 142): "Not everyone responds exactly the same way. Some will give up their houses and leave their fields. Others will offer their possessions to the community and form hospitality houses like Mary and Martha, and Peter's family.... There are the Matthews who encounter Jesus and sell everything. But then there are also the Zacchaeuses who meet Jesus and redefine their careers. So not everyone responds in the same way, but we must respond."

▌Chapter 12: Tele-vision

1. Courtesy of DreamWorks LLC and Universal Studios Licensing LLLP. *Gladiator* © DreamWorks LLC and Universal Studios. All rights reserved.

2. This is a little nerdy, but I've found at least eight examples where *tele* means "end," "completion," or "goal," including the following:

   • teleoptile – a mature feather
   • telesis – use of natural or social processes for deliberate goals
   • telestich – a poetic code using the last letter of each line
     (roughly opposite to an acrostic)

   How fascinating am I?!

3. *Chambers Concise Dictionary* (London: Chambers, 2004).

4. A great banquet (Luke 13:29); the restoration of all things (Matthew 19:28); creation released from brokenness (Romans 8:21); a fair judgement (Romans 2:6 – 11); an unfathomable mercy (Romans 11:32 – 36).

   We might find some of this future stuff hard to believe. The universe is so incomprehensibly vast, and it's the only reality we know. How could it possibly be re-created as Jesus promises? But the same point also works in reverse: if a universe this vast and complex can be created in the first place, then recreating such a universe should certainly be possible! And if anyone wants to claim that the universe came from nowhere, they're welcome to that view, but it does mean that an entire universe can spring up out of nothing. That seems to me a stranger thing to believe than the idea that a Creator God can renew a universe he has already made.

5. The first will be last (Matthew 20:16); God's alternative guest list (Matthew 5:3 – 10); the rich man's tragedy (Luke 16:19 – 31). When you read the gospels fresh it's incredible how clearly this message of reversal comes out. But many of us in wealthy consumer societies find this hard to spot because our lives are bound up with comfort, security and the status quo. To really hear what these texts want to say, we'll need all the humility and courage we can get.

6. Daniel 2:45.

7. There are many areas where collective action could make a real difference. To get involved in these issues is part of being not just a consumer but a *citizen*. A rough list might include:

   • acting to protect the environment from unsustainable consumption
   • allowing workers decent rest time
   • rescuing our politics from short-term, consumer-driven, self-interest
   • safeguarding childhood by limiting advertising aimed at children (in Sweden, for example, companies are only allowed to advertise to those over age twelve)
   • addressing the wealth gap that exacerbates consumer desire
   • pursuing fairer trade deals for developing countries
   • limiting the power of corporations to:
     – flood social space
     – take over public institutions
     – make use of labour operating on unstable contracts, unacceptably low pay or inhumane hours

8. For instance, it was once thought that the maximum amount of socially responsible investment in the UK (i.e., ethical funds) was about £2,000,000. This year it tops £6,000,000,000.

   Fairtrade tells a similar story. Early on in Fairtrade's life, one supermarket boss remarked that "only vicars would be mad enough to buy it." Currently world Fairtrade sales are worth £1,600,000,000. Either some vicars are earning a lot more than I am, or Fairtrade has gone large! It now provides a better premium to over one and a half million producers in developing countries. See *www.fairtrade.org.uk*.

9. Richard Foster, *Money, Sex and Power* (London: Hodder, 1985), 55. The great news about investing in God's kingdom is that it works proportionally. A billionaire can donate millions to charity, and it might count as only a few kingdom bonds. A homeless wanderer can share his last sip of beer, and it can count as thousands (see Luke 21:1–4). Think of it as a kingdom of God exchange rate.

10. "No Surprises," by Yorke/Greenwood/Selway/Greenwood/O'Brien © 1997 Warner/Chappell Music Ltd. (PRS). All rights reserved. Used by permission.

11. Vincent Miller, *Consuming Religion* (New York: Continuum, 2004), 123.

12. Stanley Hauerwas, "Preaching as Though We Had Enemies," *First Things* 53 (May 1995): 49.

13. Mike Riddell, *God's Home Page* (Oxford: Bible Reading Fellowship, 1998), 132–33. Ron Sider (*Rich Christians in an Age of Hunger* [London: Hodder, 1997], 78–79) is absolutely right: "When Jesus asked the rich young man to sell his goods and give to the poor, he did not say, "Become destitute and friendless." Rather, he said, 'Come, follow me.' In other words, he invited him to join a community of sharing and love … in that kind of community there would be genuine economic security."

14. William T. Cavanaugh, *Being Consumed* (Cambridge, UK: Eerdmans, 2008), 84.

15. Quoted by Marva Dawn in her truly inspirational book *Unfettered Hope* (Louisville: Westminster, 2003), 195.

▌Detox Diary

1. David Ford, *The Shape of Living* (Grand Rapids: Baker, 1997), 19.

2. Steven Bouma-Prediger, *For the Beauty of the Earth* (Grand Rapids: Baker, 2001), 21.

3. Matthew Sleeth, *Serve God, Save the Planet* (Grand Rapids: Zondervan, 2006), 91, 93.

4. Stephen Cottrell, *Do Nothing to Change Your Life* (London: Church House Publishing, 2007), 71.

5. Quoted in Dallas Willard, *The Spirit of the Disciplines* (New York: HarperCollins, 1988), 165.

Share Your Thoughts

With the Author: Your comments will be forwarded to the author when you send them to *zauthor@zondervan.com*.

With Zondervan: Submit your review of this book by writing to *zreview@zondervan.com*.

Free Online Resources at
www.zondervan.com

Zondervan AuthorTracker: Be notified whenever your favorite authors publish new books, go on tour, or post an update about what's happening in their lives at www.zondervan.com/authortracker.

Daily Bible Verses and Devotions: Enrich your life with daily Bible verses or devotions that help you start every morning focused on God. Visit www.zondervan.com/newsletters.

Free Email Publications: Sign up for newsletters on Christian living, academic resources, church ministry, fiction, children's resources, and more. Visit www.zondervan.com/newsletters.

Zondervan Bible Search: Find and compare Bible passages in a variety of translations at www.zondervanbiblesearch.com.

Other Benefits: Register yourself to receive online benefits like coupons and special offers, or to participate in research.

ZONDERVAN®

ZONDERVAN.com/
AUTHORTRACKER
follow your favorite authors